Between the Rivers

Combat Action in Iraq
2003-2005

John J. McGrath
General Editor

Combat Studies Institute Press
US Army Combined Arms Center
Fort Leavenworth, Kansas

Front cover: Soldiers from the 1st Battalion, 77th Armor Regiment, 1st Infantry Division, fight house-to-house during Operation BATON ROUGE, in Samarra, Iraq. Photo by SFC Johancharles Van Boers.

Foreword

Making history useful to the reader – this is one of the missions of the Combat Studies Institute. We strive to produce works that recount historical events to inform decision makers and to enable experiential learning. This collection of events put together by John McGrath, which occurred in Iraq during the 2003-2005 timeframe, addresses that mission.

The authors largely used primary source material - interviews and unit histories - to develop these vignettes and in doing so have made the works relatable not only to Soldiers who experienced similar situations but to any reader who can imagine themselves having to function in these types of situations.

We honor those involved in these actions and hope that by recounting their stories others may not only recognize them for their service but may also learn and grow from their experience.

CSI - The Past is Prologue!

Roderick M. Cox
Colonel, US Army
Director, Combat Studies Institute

Contents

Foreword iii

Introduction vii

The Battle of Hawijah, 7 April 2004

by John J. McGrath 1

Task Force 1-26 Infantry

 and the Easter Sunday Battle of Samarra, April 2004

by Matt M. Matthews 19

Taking it to the Enemy:

Offensive Counterinsurgency Operations,

1st Battalion, 24th Infantry, Mosul, 2004-2005

by John J. McGrath 43

Clearing the Jihad Super Bowl,

Al Qaim District, Anbar Province, November 2003

by Thomas A. Bruscino, Jr. 69

A Brigade Replaces a Division, Northern Iraq, 2004

by John McGrath 99

Glossary 123

About the Contributors 127

Maps

1. The Hawijah Area, 2004 3

2. The Battle of Hawijah, 7 April 2004 13

3. Samarra, 2004 23

4. The Western Mosul Area of Operations, 2004-2005 51

5. Plan for Action at Objective CHATTAHOOCHEE, 27 April 2005 .. 57

6. Al Qaim District, Anbar Province, Iraq 71

7. Husaybah, Iraq 75

8. 101st Airborne Division Deployment, Northern Iraq, 2003-2004 ... 103

9. Task Force Olympia Deployment in Northern Iraq, 2004 113

Introduction

This work is the continuation and revision of a project started in 2006 with the publication of *In Contact!* by the Combat Studies Institute. The original concept was to present a series of military vignettes in a style similar to the widely used case-study methodology commonly found in military literature. The final version of *Between the Rivers*, instead of following this strict case-study format, presents combat action vignettes as narrative accounts of the various types of actions challenging combat leaders in Iraq in 2003-2005.

The use of military case studies was common in the pre-World War I German *Kriegsakademie,* the school that trained General Staff officers. Training exercises, either in a classroom setting or in the field, were often stopped in order to make students devise solutions to a combat dilemma a commander or staff officer would be expected to face in a future war. Similarly, the Germans intensely studied military history and used historical vignettes in the training of officers. After World War I, the interwar Reichswehr made extensive study of the war, attempting to discover and codify the lessons of the war. One of the commercial products of this field of study was then-Colonel Erwin Rommel's publication of his World War I memoirs, *Infantry Attacks*, in 1937. Rommel wrote his memoirs as a series of case studies that presented the lessons of the war based on his own experiences.

The German experience interfaced with the United States Army when German Army CPT Adolf von Schell, a World War I infantry veteran and General Staff officer, who attended the advanced course for infantry officers at the US Army Infantry School in 1930-31 as part of an extended visit to the United States, which also included an internship under Henry Ford. Schell, later a general in the World War II Wehrmacht, gave a series of lectures in a case-study format to the other students based on his wartime experiences. The lectures so impressed the staff of the Infantry School that they were privately published by the local newspaper, *The Benning Herald*, in 1933 under the title *Battle Leadership*. The book is still in print. Schell's example motivated two officers at the Infantry School, COL George C. Marshall and MAJ Forrest Harding, to develop an American version of Schell's book, a much more extensive volume published in 1934, *Infantry in Battle*. Consisting of a large number of case studies drawn primarily from the American experience in World War I, the volume represented an effort to bridge the well-known gap between peacetime training experience and the reality of combat. Designed as a text for use in the Army school system, the *Infantry in Battle* case studies offered officers a way to prepare themselves vicariously for future wars based on the experiences of the recent past. The format proved so popular that the work quickly became a classic. Its form has been replicated in large measure by a work of the same title published in 2005 by the Infantry School, which draws on vignettes from the ongoing war on terrorism. Earlier, in 1992 the Combat Studies Institute produced a similar successor volume, *Combined Arms in Battle Since1939*, which expanded the original concept to other combat branches.

Following World War II, the War Department Historical Division in 1946 published *Small Unit Actions*, the study of some discrete battles drawn from three different theaters of war. While the educational motive was present to some degree, the primary purpose of this volume was to explain to all, public and Soldiers alike, what the recent war looked like at battalion level and below. In 1954, following the Korean War, the Office of the Chief of Military History, United States Army, published *Combat Actions in Korea*. Consisting of descriptions of 19 small-unit actions, this substantial volume found its primary justification as an educational tool for those who had not experienced the events described. Fully annotated, each chapter consisted of a colorful narrative followed by an analytical discussion of salient points. Nearly 20 years later, toward the end of American combat in Vietnam, the Office of the Chief of Military History again essayed to address small-unit actions with the publication of *Seven Firefights in Vietnam*. This work aspired only to provide straightforward narratives that were representative of the types of combat American soldiers had encountered in that conflict. Based on primary sources, but without annotation in the published version, the chapters were also devoid of overt analysis, which was left to the reader.

In tandem with official products, journalist-turned US Army combat historian S.L.A. Marshall began producing a series of commercial publications presenting small-unit case studies starting with World War II and continuing through the Korean War, the 1956 Arab-Israeli conflicts, and Vietnam. Marshall developed a group interview technique that attempted to produce an accurate narrative account of complicated small-unit actions. His methodology and interpretation of events have been criticized in recent years, but his influence on the US Army cannot be disputed. Current military history detachments often conduct group interviews based on the guidelines Marshall established. In terms of case-study methodology, his works present a parallel progression in the development of the military case study and were and are widely read by military professionals.

The present volume lies directly within the tradition of these predecessor works on small-unit actions. Since the fall of 2001, the United States Army, along with the other American armed services, has been engaged in military actions in Iraq and Afghanistan. Because the current conflict has so many different fronts and facets, no handful of small- unit case studies could do justice to such a complex tapestry of events. This book thus represents a volume that showcases the American soldier in combat operations within the context of the Global War on Terrorism/The Long War. This series of five case studies is drawn from events in Iraq. Four of the studies discuss combat operations within a counterinsurgency framework at the company and battalion levels. The final case study presents a deployment dilemma facing a brigade-level task force commander when he was asked to replace a whole division in the same geographical space. In each case, the story is derived from oral interviews and key documents and is fully annotated. The primary purpose for presenting these vignettes is to provide a vicarious education in what future participants will face as the War on Terrorism continues and beyond.

The scholarship for the current work was produced in 2006 and 2007. Its revival as a publication lies directly with the efforts of COL Roderick Cox, CSI Director. Also needing acknowledgement for their essential roles in the production of this volume are Dr. Donald Wright, editor Terry England, and Dr. Anthony Carlson, who assisted with the historical editing.

December 2012

The Battle of Hawijah
7 April 2004

by

John J. McGrath

On 7 April 2004 in Iraq countrywide disturbances were in their fourth day. The Shiite Mahdi Army led the unrest in the Sadr City district of Baghdad and in the cities of Karbala, Najaf, Kufa, Kut, Nasiriyah, Amara, and Basra. Fierce fighting with Sunni insurgents was also taking place in Fallujah, Ramadi, and Baquba. On this Saturday the strife spread to additional Sunni areas, including the city of Hawijah, located in Tamim Province, 130 miles north of Baghdad.

Hawijah is situated approximately 40 miles southwest of Kirkuk, and several miles north of the major oil pipeline running from Kirkuk to Bayji, the refinery city on the Tigris River. The inhabitants of this area are almost entirely Sunni Arab and the population in 2004 was about 70,000. Although there was little insurgent activity in the area prior to April 2004, Hawijah was long recognized as both a Baathist and a fundamental Islamic stronghold.[1]

In April 2004, the local US Army forces were part of the 2d Brigade, 25th Infantry Division, from the second American troop rotation in Tamim Province, a unit which was based out of Kirkuk. The brigade was a light infantry force out of Schofield Barracks, Hawaii, which had originally been slated for deployment to Afghanistan. Shortfalls in Coalition support diverted the light infantrymen to central Iraq. The brigade deployed in January 2004. By early April, the officers and soldiers had over two months experience in combat and contingency operations in the area.[2]

Specific responsibility for the large area southwest of Kirkuk, including Hawijah, belonged to the 1st Battalion, 27th Infantry (1-27 IN), the Wolfhounds. The battalion operated out of Forward Operating Base (FOB) McHenry, located two miles southeast of the center of Hawijah, just north of the road running out of Hawijah to the southeast that joined the Kirkuk- Bayji oil pipeline. The FOB was in the middle of an expanse of land cleared for agriculture that made it easily defendable. Each of the three companies in the 1-27 IN had specific sector responsibilities within the battalion's 144 square kilometer area of responsibility (AOR). A (Alpha) Company, commanded by CPT Scott W. Carpenter, had the largest and most densely populated AOR — the city of Hawijah itself.[3]

After a brief skirmish on its very first day in Hawijah in February, the Wolfhound battalion had faced a relatively quiet situation. Until early April, the Sunni population was not restive, unlike the situation in other parts of Iraq, particularly in Anbar Province and in Baghdad. Despite this, A Company remained alert, using this period to become familiar with the local population and the geography of the city.[4]

It was in this quiet climate that Carpenter went to the city on the morning of 7 April. In fulfilling his responsibilities, the company commander routinely coordinated or supported the development and activities of local Iraqi officials, particularly the appointed civil city council, the police force, and the 207th Battalion of the Iraqi Civil Defense Corps (ICDC). The latter organization was stationed in a barracks compound in the eastern-center of Hawijah next to the City Council Building. One of Carpenter's duties was to attend and monitor the city council's weekly meeting. Therefore, at about 0945 hours on the morning of 7 April 2004, accompanied by two squads from his 2d Platoon, he left FOB McHenry and moved to the ICDC Compound in the city. Upon reaching the city from the east, the company commander discovered that a downtown protest march of roughly 150 individuals was taking place along the main east-west thoroughfare, Market Street, which ran in front of both the City Council Building and the ICDC compound. The protest march was moving west to east and arrived at the ICDC directly after Carpenter's detachment entered the compound. The leader of the protest, an unidentified male, stood up on the small wall surrounding the municipal building and began speaking to the crowd as Carpenter went into the building from a side entrance to attend the council meeting.[5]

Various factors effectively reduced Carpenter's combat power. The first was organizational. The 1-27 IN had replaced a mechanized infantry battalion from the 4th Infantry Division (Mechanized). Although the 1-27 IN was given the same sector, the previous unit had contained numerous armored and wheeled vehicles as part of its organizational structure and, thus, was able to cover a wider area with vehicles suitable for combat operations.

However, 1-27 IN was a light infantry unit. By organization, each company had a single high mobility multipurpose wheeled vehicle (HMMWV) equipped with a digital communications package and thin armored plating. Once in Iraq, the company picked up an additional nine cargo HMMWVs upon which platoons placed their M240 machine guns, some with vehicle mounts and others without. Over time, these vehicles received armored plating made by local contractors. Because of the relatively large area of responsibility, the infantry patrolled and moved around the operational area in less capable vehicles. Geography and equipment accordingly dispersed Carpenter's combat power.[6]

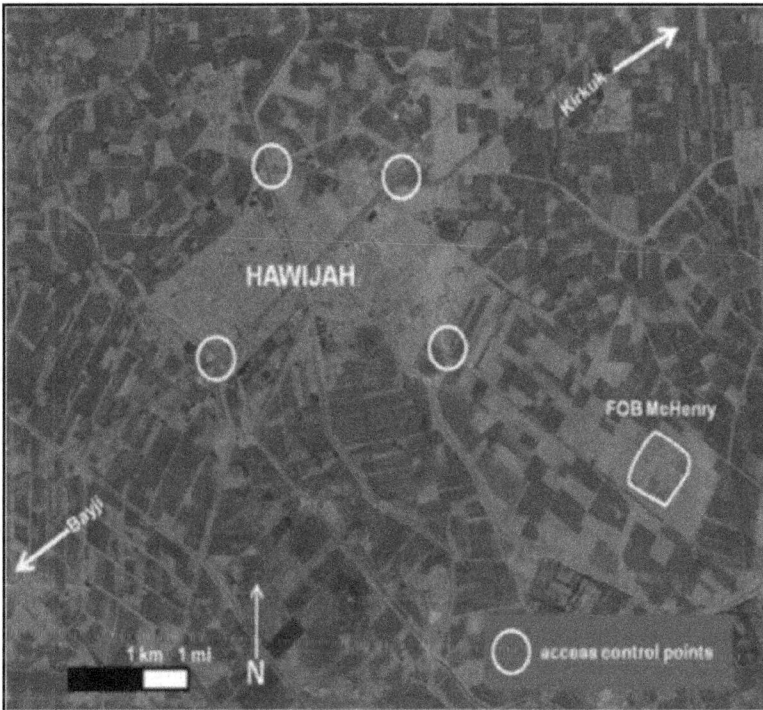

Map 1. The Hawijah Area, 2004.

The second limiting factor was operational. Carpenter's company was part of the garrison of FOB McHenry. One of his three platoons rotated through security duties at the FOB. To standardize this duty, the company commander established a triple rotation system. One platoon was on combat alert for 24 hours and conducted any required operational assignments. A second platoon was on stand-down, recovering from its alert shift for a period of 24 hours. The third platoon was on FOB guard detail. Carpenter implemented this rotation plan not only to fulfill operational and mission requirements, but to keep his troops fresh and lessen the enemy's ability to discern patterns of behavior. Company A also provided a platoon on a rotational basis to serve as the battalion's quick reaction force (QRF).

On 7 April, B Company was providing this platoon, which was based out of FOB McHenry. This system meant that Carpenter generally had only a platoon-sized element for daily combat operations in and around Hawijah.[7]

3

Routine security in Hawijah was an Iraqi police responsibility. The police station was located in the eastern center of the city, around the corner from the municipal building and ICDC compound. Geography made securing the city from the outside relatively simple. While located on a relatively open agricultural plain, Hawijah was, nevertheless, isolated from the countryside by a series of canals that ran completely around the edge of the city. This moat-like effect restricted access to the city to four main roads. Checkpoints, manned by the Hawijah police force, covered all four of these entrances.

While covering the four entrances to the city with checkpoints isolated it from the outside, the city was further compartmentalized into two sections by a canal running north-south through its center. There were north-south roads running parallel to this canal on both its eastern and western sides. However, crossings over the canal were limited. Vehicular traffic could only cross the canal to enter the opposite half of the city via three bridges. A fourth bridge only allowed pedestrians. Control of these central bridges was essential to the success of any combat operation in the city.[8]

From the ICDC compound, Carpenter could observe the marchers on Market Street assembled in front of the municipal building. The ICDC commander had told him that the parade was a peaceful student protest. The grounds of the local university were located just to the northeast. While the mob seemed peaceful, they displayed various signs and chanted slogans showing sympathy for both the Shiite Mahdi Army and the Sunni defenders of Fallujah, a city that harbored insurgents and was under attack by Coalition forces in early April 2004. This indicated to Carpenter that the crowd probably consisted of outside agitators. If so, this implied that one of the external city checkpoints had been compromised. Seemingly an Iraqi sympathizer had allowed hostile, though peaceful, Iraqi demonstrators to enter the city proper. If peaceful outsiders had made their way into the city, the possibility existed that non-peaceful forces had also come into the city. If it came to a direct confrontation, Carpenter had only a small force with him — part of the company headquarters element and most of the 2d Platoon, with three HMMWVs, two of which had machine guns. While this force was probably large enough to secure the ICDC compound and the adjoining municipal building if the mob became unruly, would it be adequate in size to confront simultaneously both the protesters, if they became unruly, and fight armed insurgents seeking to gain control of the city center, if such a group appeared? This question troubled Carpenter.[9]

4

As he prepared to go into the city council meeting, the A Company commander had several options to resolve the situation. He could cancel the council meeting and coordinate with the local Iraqi commander to find out where the crowd came from, while informing his battalion commander of the situation. By cancelling the meeting, Carpenter could avoid an immediate confrontation with hostile Iraqis, while possibly discovering the origin of a security leak. However, it could give the hostile faction a moral victory. Additionally, Carpenter would still find himself in the middle of an intimidating crowd with a small force. In any pitched battle, he realized that the 207th ICDC Battalion, greatly under strength and poorly trained, would be capable only of defending its own compound. The Iraqi police, similarly, would have their hands full defending their own nearby police station.[10]

Carpenter could force an immediate confrontation with the crowd to clear Market Street. Such a move would immediately clear the downtown area, but could also cause a premature and, possibly, unnecessary confrontation. Without reinforcement, the American force would remain small; adding to the risk but it could also head off further trouble before it started.

Carpenter could also conduct the meeting as usual and keep the second platoon on alert and in a security posture looking for the appearance of any insurgents. At the same time, Carpenter could call for reinforcements from the battalion QRF, giving him a larger force to face any possible confrontation after the meeting.

CPT Carpenter chose to hold the meeting as scheduled and called for the battalion QRF, a platoon from B Company, to be sent immediately to the city. With reinforcements on the way, he attended the meeting with his company FIST chief, 1LT Robert J. Heatherly, who also acted as the company's civil affairs officer. While the meeting progressed as normal, the squads of the 2d Platoon, led by 1LT Gary Kaldahl, provided internal security of the municipal building and overlooked the general area around the building from its roof.[11]

A half hour into the council meeting, Carpenter heard gunfire from the roof of the building. He immediately adjourned the meeting allowing the nervous council members to leave a location they felt had become a target. As he left, Carpenter discovered that one of his snipers was engaging an insurgent armed with a rocket-propelled grenade launcher several blocks away. With his small command-post group (including 1LT Heatherly and Carpenter's RTO, SPC Robert H. Chapman), he moved to the roof to find out what was going on.

During the course of the meeting, 1LT Kaldahl had relocated one of his snipers, SPC Roberto Zuniga-Saucedo, to the northwest corner of the roof of the two-story municipal building to observe the cityscape for hostile forces. A squad led by SSG Andrew W. Gregory, conducted similar duty along the southern edge of the roof. After some time, Zuniga observed a man armed with an RPG-7 launcher hiding in the shadows around the corner of a side street on the northern side of Market Street, several blocks west of the municipal building. The sniper engaged the RPG gunner with his M14 sniper rifle and continued firing single rounds at the figure until he incapacitated him with a wound to the arm. The situation on Market Street below sorted itself out. With the sound of Zuniga's first shot, the crowd immediately dispersed, leaving only insurgents and American soldiers in the Market Street area.[12]

Although the crowd was gone, additional enemy combatants began appearing to the west and south. First, Gregory's squad and Carpenter's command post began taking small arms fire from a building 200 to 250 meters to the south of the ICDC compound. Gregory returned fire and in response the enemy shot an RPG rocket that went high and exploded into a house north of Market Street.[13]

The battalion QRF, B Company's 1st Platoon under 1LT Christopher Johnson, arrived on Market Street at the ICDC compound mounted in two HMMWVs, having taken the eastern route. Although expecting to provide security for the government buildings against a civilian crowd, as the QRF, Johnson realized he had to be ready for anything. The platoon reached the ICDC compound just as Zuniga's firing dispersed the crowd. To the men of Johnson's platoon, it seemed like the crowd disappeared as soon as they appeared. For a minute the city seemed to become a ghost town. However, this was only an illusion. A number of insurgents appeared from windows and corners in the general vicinity of where Zuniga had shot the RPG gunner. With Market Street now clear, these enemy fighters began firing volleys of RPG rockets at the new arrivals. The QRF took cover and returned fire, initially taking no casualties. Carpenter was now in a fight.[14]

After reporting the situation to the battalion tactical operations center (TOC) at FOB McHenry, relayed through his vehicle's digitized communications package, he requested additional forces and the battalion released to him his company's 1st Platoon, which had been in reserve at FOB McHenry recovering from recent operations. The platoon began moving to Hawijah under the leadership of 2LT David S. Morgan. The company executive officer, 1LT Christopher A. Hopes, and the acting first sergeant, SFC Steven Green, accompanied the platoon to the city.[15]

With more forces on the way, Carpenter decided to act offensively and use the QRF platoon against the enemy forces on Market Street to push them back against the canal in the center of the city. While his 2d Platoon would support this maneuver by fire while continuing to secure the ICDC compound and municipal building, he would use any reinforcements to apply additional offensive combat power against the insurgent forces.[16]

The QRF force advanced slowly down Market Street to the west while under heavy but inaccurate RPG and small arms fire. Platoon leader Johnson originally envisioned advancing the platoon in three squads, one directly down Market Street, and the other two on the north and south sides of the main street, respectively. The northern squad would also contain the platoon's two HMMWVs with machine guns mounted on them, and would support the advance of the squad on Market Street.[17]

That squad, led by SSG Victor Benavides, advanced west on Market with its initial objective being the first four-corner intersection beyond the municipal building. However, Benavides quickly became pinned down by enemy fire and had to be reinforced by the firepower of the rest of the platoon to continue the advance. The platoon suffered the first American casualty of the day when CPL Clint Davis was wounded in the leg and shoulder while crossing Market Street. His comrades had to drag Davis out of enemy fire, after which Carpenter promptly had the wounded noncommissioned officer evacuated to the ICDC compound.[18]

At the first crossroads, Johnson's platoon faced fire from three directions. Benavides received a head wound from small-arms fire. His Kevlar helmet stopped the round and the stunned squad leader was soon back in action. Platoon sergeant, SFC Eugene Dydasco, brought up the platoon's two HMMWVs. The additional firepower allowed the advance to begin again. Moving door-to-door along buildings on both sides of Market Street, the platoon advanced to the canal.[19]

Carpenter now faced the decision of how to deploy and use the reinforcing platoon on its way from FOB McHenry. To facilitate his understanding of the situation, he had moved from the roof of the municipal building to the ICDC compound from where he could see the action taking place along Market Street. He then moved behind Johnson's platoon, observing their firefight.[19]

The A Company commander decided initially to bring the new platoon to the central location of the ICDC compound and from there determine its best employment. He had several choices for the use of the platoon. One of these would be to reinforce the two platoons on Market Street. The increase in combat power could result in the infliction of decisive damage on the insurgents being pushed towards the central city canal bottleneck. Additionally, Carpenter felt that if push came to shove, he could get additional combat assets from those at FOB McHenry if the enemy proved to be in large numbers.

He could also employ the platoon against the insurgents located to the south of the ICDC compound. While this would separate the company into two distinct elements, increasing command and control difficulties, it would also provide flank security for the forces on Market Street. However, such a move was risky in that enemy dispositions and force size to the south was unknown. The new platoon could end up taking on a "tiger by the tail."

A similar risky course of action would be to shift the new platoon around the Market Street battle and place it in blocking positions along the canal at the bridges. The unknown enemy situation — and there were indications that there were insurgents firing across the canal from the western half of the city — made the movement of a small platoon unsupported into a different section of the city very dangerous but, if the platoon was able to successfully block the canal, the enemy forces in the eastern half of the city could potentially be completely destroyed.[20]

Finally, Carpenter could retain the platoon as a reserve at the ICDC compound. This option had the advantage of providing flexibility in case new enemy forces appeared or the insurgents to the south began threatening the flank of the Market Street forces. However, creation of such a reserve also would leave the company with the combat power of only two platoons fighting the enemy.

Carpenter chose to use his reinforcements to reinforce the Market Street battle. En route to the ICDC compound, A Company's 1st Platoon, with the company executive officer and first sergeant in tow, encountered a wire obstacle placed across Market Street blocking the eastern approaches to Hawijah to the east of where the two platoons were fighting. While the obstacle was only a minor nuisance, its presence showed that the enemy was conducting a coordinated operation, part of which was designed to hinder the arrival of American reinforcements.[21]

Upon arrival at the ICDC compound, Carpenter ordered 2LT Morgan to take his platoon down the opposite (northern) side of Market Street and reinforce the B Company platoon. He then took his command-post group and accompanied the platoon down to the B Company platoon's position, three blocks west of the ICDC compound. The platoons in contact were now taking heavy machine gun and RPG fire and, in addition to CPL Davis from Johnson's platoon, the reinforcing platoon had also received its first casualties. Carpenter established a casualty collection point at the ICDC compound, using his command HMMWV to evacuate the first casualties. With the first wounded, he called the battalion TOC and requested the dispatch of another infantry platoon to operate against the right (southern) flank on the insurgents on Market Street and possibly prevent their egress across the canal bridges.[22]

Carpenter soon had cause to reflect on the wisdom of his decision to reinforce the Market Street axis. Enemy forces to the north began firing into the right flank of the company's advance from several side streets. Carpenter himself and his CP group were under direct fire and forced to take cover and, subsequently, to cover the evacuation of a wounded A Company noncommissioned officer. By voice command, Carpenter directed 2LT Morgan to send a squad up the street from which the fire was coming in order to suppress it. Fire Team Leader SGT Don K. Wegesend led the advance of that unit, SSG Chad C. Borcher's 1st Squad, 1st Platoon. The squad advanced tactically up the street one block to the first intersection north of Market Street. However, before it could advance farther, Wegesend was wounded in the arm by fire from the far (western) corner of the next intersection. The CP group, using its up-armored HMMWV, moved to the team's location and evacuated the wounded noncommissioned officer while Carpenter stayed with the squad.[23]

While observing Borcher's advance, Johnson notified him that his platoon had reached the canal. With Johnson at the canal and Morgan advancing to the north, Carpenter was faced with the decision of what to do next. He had also asked for and would soon receive additional forces. The battalion commander had released his 3d Platoon, led by 1LT Timothy Ungaro, formerly on security detail at FOB McHenry. He needed to instruct Ungaro on where to go. With four platoons in the action, Carpenter needed to coordinate their activity. Johnson and Morgan were essentially operating independent of each other. The company commander needed to devise a scheme of maneuver in which each platoon's actions operated in support of both the other platoons and the company as a whole, with the goal of destroying the insurgent forces in Hawijah.

With two platoons in contact, one providing security at the ICDC compound, and a fourth on its way to the city, Carpenter had a certain tactical flexibility. However, he felt that it was too risky to shift Kaldahl's under strength platoon away from the ICDC compound. His actions would be predicated on the employment of the two platoons facing the enemy and the one reinforcing. Carpenter could use the platoons to keep pushing the enemy to their front into the western half of the city, then sweeping through that half of the town. Morgan's platoon would advance and pursue the insurgents to its front and secure the northern vehicular bridge and the footbridge to the south of it. Johnson, already at the Market Street crossing of the canal, would cross the bridge there and clear the insurgents to his front to the western limits of the city. Ungaro's reinforcing platoon would move along the southern axis, crossing the canal at the southern bridge and clear the most southerly portion of western Hawijah.

This alternative was the simplest to execute and, if successful, could relentlessly push the enemy out into the open area west of the city where Apaches could destroy the insurgents. However, this selection gave one platoon (Morgan's) the mission of both securing the northern exit from the city and clearing the northwestern quarter. The task could be too much for a single platoon. Since this part of the city was the farthest from FOB McHenry, it was also the farthest from reinforcement.

To alleviate this potential threat, Carpenter could reinforce the northern area by moving Johnson's platoon northerly along the canal from Market Street to the northern bridge. This platoon could both cover the northern approaches to the city (left unsecured by the Iraqi police) and the advance of Morgan's platoon across the canal into northwest Hawijah. Morgan could advance across the footbridge south of the northernmost vehicular bridge while Johnson's men covered the platoon's right flank. Farther to the south, Ungaro's fresh platoon could then advance along either the Market Street central axis or across the southern bridge to clear southwest Hawijah.

By doing so, however, Carpenter would leave the southern area vulnerable. He probably needed a minimum of two platoons to effectively cover both southern routes. However, this area was the closest to FOB McHenry and the A Company commander could reasonably expect additional reinforcements, which could arrive quickly. While the vulnerability existed, the risk was a lot less than under-manning the northern area. Apart from this there were several advantages in this option. It allowed the two platoons in contact to mutually support each other, while allowing the new platoon to get into action as quickly as possible. Using a platoon at all bridges except the one nearest reinforcements, would allow a simultaneous multi-platoon sweep across the west side of the city which could force the enemy out into the open areas west and north of the city, where the insurgents would be easy prey for the Apaches.

Carpenter decided to reinforce the northern area with Johnson's platoon. He ordered Johnson to turn northward along the canal's eastern side and advance up to the northern vehicular bridge. Morgan was to continue pressing the enemy in his sector, cross the footbridge and push to the northwest. Ungaro was to advance against the southernmost bridge and cross to the western side of the city. Morgan and Ungaro's units would then advance westward, clearing the insurgents from the city to the west.[24]

The operation did not exactly work out as planned. Ungaro found it impossible to advance on the southern bridge because the battalion commander tasked him to escort the battalion command sergeant major, CSM Karl K. Morgan, and a medical section of two frontline ambulances (FLAs). Ungaro felt it was prudent to bring the medics and Morgan to Carpenter's position along Market Street behind Johnson's platoon. However, Ungaro's arrival in the center rather than in the south forced him to modify his maneuver. While the CSM supervised the evacuation of casualties first to the ICDC compound and then back to FOB McHenry, Carpenter decided it was best to employ Ungaro's 3d Platoon on the Market Street axis, which Johnson's platoon was preparing to leave to head north along the canal. The decision was simplified when he received word that another platoon from B Company was being dispatched from FOB McHenry. Carpenter gave the new platoon Ungaro's former mission of advancing across the southernmost bridge.

Meanwhile, in response to Carpenter's previous instructions, 2LT Morgan had divided his platoon up by squads. Two squads, Borcher's previously mentioned 1st, and SSG Allen E. West's 2d Squad, 1st Platoon, advanced to the north on city streets perpendicular to Market Street and a block apart. While moving forward, each squad had a sergeant team leader wounded by enemy fire. The squads were operating against small insurgent elements employing machine guns and RPGs. Morgan accompanied West's squad. His third squad reinforced the B Company platoon at the canal bridge until it shifted to the north, and then followed the rest of its own platoon. The enemy began falling back in front of Morgan's squads.[25]

With Carpenter's command group nearby, Borcher's squad maneuvered against an insurgent RPG position and managed to surprise the enemy and kill the entire four-man team. Carpenter then directed Borcher to coordinate his advance with West and Morgan. Using his vehicular communications system, the company commander coordinated to complete his plan for the destruction of the enemy. The battalion S-3 authorized his use of fire from several Apache helicopters that came up from Tikrit and were now on station to support the maneuver of the ground forces.

Carpenter gave the aviators a free hand by directing that the helicopters fire at any visible insurgent positions or groups west of the 1st Platoon's advancing squads. To facilitate coordination, Carpenter popped a smoke grenade to give the aviators a rough idea of the forward edge of friendly positions. Ultimately, while the attack helicopters remained on station for the rest of the battle, no enemy targets appeared as the enemy went to ground and the Apaches were never used.[26]

Carpenter instructed Ungaro to move west down Market Street and cross the canal bridge and close with the enemy forces on the west side, clearing them along that axis to the western edge of the city. The additional B Company platoon would at the same time cross the southern bridge and advance to the left (south) of Ungaro, clearing enemy forces along a parallel axis.[27]

Simultaneous to these movements, the 1st Platoon (Morgan) was already clearing along a northwesterly axis to the north of Market Street. Carpenter's intent was that the combined effect of these platoon movements would force the enemy into the northwestern corner of the city, where they would either have to stand and fight, or escape into open agricultural land beyond the city, where the Apaches could destroy them.[28]

Morgan's unit began to take additional casualties. The platoon, led by Borcher's squad on the left, had crossed the footbridge over the central canal into the western half of the city. Borcher was pursuing a group of insurgents into a west-side industrial area. There the enemy sprung an ambush, firing a volley of three RPG rockets at the squad. One rocket missed, another failed to detonate, but a third exploded into the middle of SGT Jay R. Lawrence's fire team, wounding Lawrence in the arm, SPC Ryan J. Geode in the head, and PFC David L. Goodwin in the leg. The action took place close to the family residence of the industrial park's security guard, whose young daughter also was wounded by shrapnel from the RPG round. The proximity of noncombatant civilians to their ambush site was obviously not an enemy concern.[29]

Carpenter decided to use his CP vehicle with its armor to evacuate the casualties. SSG Borcher was unsure of the squad's exact location. The CP group used a water tower Borcher could see from his location to provide a bearing. The HMMWV crossed the canal and approached the water tower. Thick metal fencing compartmentalized the open industrial area. Therefore, when Carpenter's group found Borcher's location, the vehicle had to take a roundabout route to reach the wounded soldiers. Upon reaching the squad's position, the wounded fire team was loaded onto the vehicle. At the same time the bulk of the 1st Platoon arrived at the location, accompanied by 1LT Hopes, the company executive officer, with his HMMWV. The CP group trans loaded the casualties, including the little girl, into the executive officer's truck, which then evacuated them.[30]

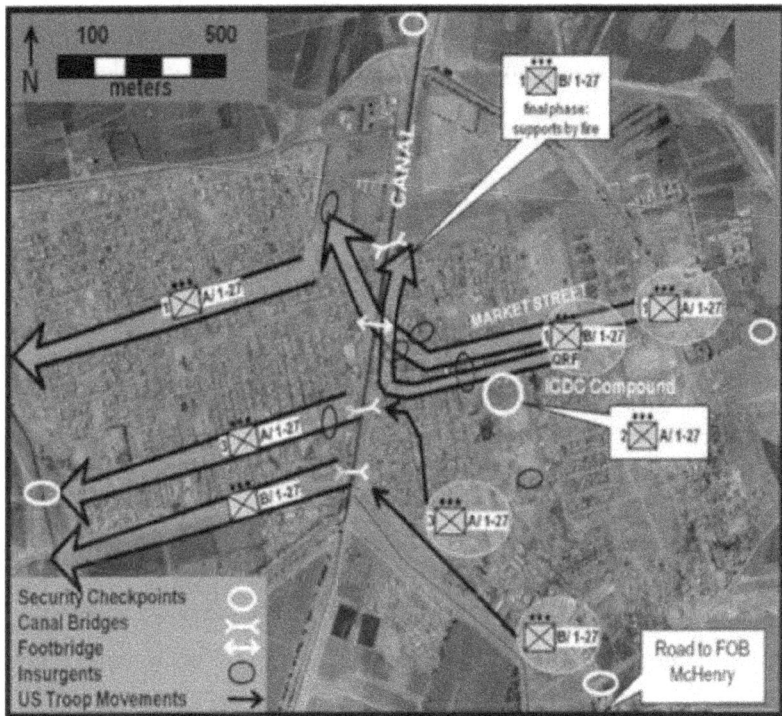

Map 2. The Battle of Hawijah, 7 April 2004.

Meanwhile, along Market Street, Ungaro crossed the canal bridge and began advancing westerly, parallel to the other B company platoon to the south. Johnson's 1st Platoon (B Company) moved to the northernmost bridge and began over watching to the north and west. The net effect of these movements was the defeat of the insurgents. After the RPG ambush of Lawrence's fire team, firing throughout the city petered out. Each platoon continued its advance to the western edges of the built-up area unopposed. The enemy had broken up into groups of individuals and had gone to ground within the urban landscape.[31]

At the ICDC compound, 1LT Kaldahl's 2d Platoon continued to provide security. Kaldahl's men had been engaging in a long-range firefight with insurgents in the southeastern quadrant of the city. 2d Platoon firepower had long suppressed the enemy's RPG and machine gun fire. When fighting died out in the western districts, the enemy to the south faded away and disappeared into the city.[32]

13

Accordingly, Carpenter directed his A Company task force to begin the clearing of individual buildings from which enemy fire had been observed in the western half of the city, but which had been bypassed in the advance. The search discovered several small weapons caches and detained numerous adult males. At the end of the day, US forces had completely secured Hawijah. The result of the action on 7 April 2004 was a complete American victory. The Wolfhounds had killed 35 enemy combatants, wounded an additional 45 insurgents, and detained 58 others, while suffering six soldiers and one noncombatant wounded. At the end of the day, A Company retained complete control of Hawijah.[33]

Although the battle of 7 April was the largest commitment of enemy forces in Hawijah up to that time, at no point did the insurgents assemble a force anywhere that was strong enough to threaten the survival of any A Company platoon or squad. At no time during the battle did the Wolfhounds not have fire superiority on the streets of the city. This mismatch allowed Carpenter to maneuver his forces in such a way as to maximize damage to the insurgents.[34]

In retrospect it appears likely that the insurgent force in Hawijah was arraying itself to conduct a coordinated attack from all directions against the US forces near the ICDC compound. Similar to other attacks around Iraq at the time, the enemy probably intended to capture the Hawijah government buildings and sack them. The attack was to be taped for dissemination to media outlets friendly to the insurgent cause. The cameraman was, however, captured by the A Company executive officer, 1LT Hopes. The tape included scenes of the demonstration, which was obviously being used as a cover for the insurgent gunmen to move into their pre-attack positions. Perhaps the enemy also hoped the demonstrators would provoke a bloody confrontation that would provide both an excuse for their subsequent attack and provide a propaganda victory through pre-staged video of noncombatant casualties.

Enemy expectations of American reactions were off the mark. US forces did not attack the demonstrators, nor did they stand by and await an insurgent attack. From previous enemy activities elsewhere in Iraq in the preceding days, Carpenter felt the government buildings were the enemy's attack objective. He centered his offensive operations from a secure base at this probable insurgent objective. Meanwhile, his troops employed active security measures, remained alert, and sought any early signs of insurgent activity. The sniper's action against an enemy combatant scattered the crowd and forced the enemy into premature initiation of their attack. Since Carpenter had already requested reinforcements, the first group arrived before the enemy could block their route and were able to react immediately to the dangerous situation and seize the initiative from the enemy.

Carpenter used his knowledge of Hawijah geography, gained over the previous two months, in order to direct the movements of his subordinate elements. The limited entrances into the city and the bottlenecks at the bridges along the canal running laterally through the center of the city made enemy movements and reactions relatively predictable, allowing friendly forces to maximize combat power at the optimum places.

US forces arrived piecemeal in a series of platoon reinforcements. Given the vague enemy situation and the compartmentalization of combat power within 1-27 IN because of multiple operational and administrative requirements, this was virtually unavoidable. However, the timing of the reinforcements helped Carpenter refine his maneuver based on the tactical situation. This culminated in a complete defeat for the overmatched insurgents.

Carpenter coordinated the activities of up to five platoons and Apache support helicopters while moving around the battlefield in his armored HMMWV, placing himself at key locations. The company's shortage of vehicles that could operate under enemy fire forced him to use his vehicle for casualty evacuation when necessary. Evacuation did not become a tactical distraction primarily because of the relatively small number of American and noncombatant casualties.

Iraqi ICDC and police forces played no role in the Hawijah action. The police abandoned the four checkpoints controlling access to the city and moved to their station where they remained throughout the battle. The ICDC forces also remained in their compound. In 2004, both of these forces were new organizations and relatively untrained. This provides the context for the great strides made in subsequent years with the Iraqi Security Forces (ISF) throughout Iraq, and in Hawijah in particular. By early 2008, the former 207th ICDC Battalion, redesignated as 1st Battalion, 2d Brigade, 4th Iraqi Army Division, assumed complete responsibility for security and combat operations in Hawijah. The unit's performance had so improved that it received the honorific title of "Lion Battalion."[35]

The battle on 7 April 2004 was the first and only large fight in Hawijah. Except for a skirmish on 11 November 2004, the city remained relatively calm throughout 1-27 IN's tour. Wolfhound forces faced minor IED or RPG ambushes and the threat of a skillful enemy sharpshooter dubbed the "Hawijah sniper," who caused several casualties but there were no insurgent actions on the scale of that attempted on 7 April 2004.[36]

Notes

1. Nadra Saouli, "Northern Coalition Fighting US Troops in Kirkuk: Officials of Ousted Baath Regime Join Forces with Islamists to Attack US Troops in Northern Iraq," *Middle East Online*, 4 December 2003, online at http://www. middle- east-online.com/english/?id=8039, accessed on 3 April 2008.

2. MAJ Scott Carpenter, interview by David Kunselman, 23 August 2007, Fort Leavenworth, 4-5.

3. Carpenter interview; MAJ Scott Carpenter, interview by author, 26 March 2008.

4. Carpenter interview, 23 August 2007.

5. CPT Scott Carpenter, "The Battle of Huwayjah," 8 April 2004, unpublished manuscript in author's possession; Carpenter interview, 23 August 2007.

6. Carpenter interview, 23 August 2007.

7. Carpenter interview, 23 August 2007

8. Carpenter interview, 23 August 2007

9. Carpenter interview, 23 August 2007

10. Carpenter interview, 23 August 2007

11. Carpenter, "The Battle of Huwayjah."

12. Carpenter, "The Battle of Huwayjah."; Carpenter interview, 23 August 2007.

13. Carpenter, "The Battle of Huwayjah."

14. Discovery Channel, "Ambush at Hawijah, April 7, 2004," *Combat Zone*, Episode 10, 2007.

15. Carpenter, "The Battle of Huwayjah."

16. Carpenter, "The Battle of Huwayjah."

17. "Ambush at Hawijah," April 7, 2004.

18. "Ambush at Hawijah," April 7, 2004; MAJ Scott Carpenter, interview by the author, 2 April 2008.

19. Carpenter, "The Battle of Huwayjah."

20. Carpenter, "The Battle of Huwayjah."

21. Carpenter, "The Battle of Huwayjah."; CPT Scott Carpenter, "The Battle of Hawijah, 8 April 2004 LPD," PowerPoint Briefing, 3 October 2005, in author's possession.

22. Carpenter, "The Battle of Huwayjah."

23. Carpenter, "The Battle of Huwayjah."; Carpenter, PowerPoint Briefing.

24. Carpenter, "The Battle of Huwayjah;" Carpenter interview, 2 April 2008.

25. Carpenter, "The Battle of Huwayjah."

26. Carpenter, "The Battle of Huwayjah;" Carpenter interview, 2 April 2008

27. Carpenter, "The Battle of Huwayjah."

28. Carpenter, "The Battle of Huwayjah."

29. Carpenter, "The Battle of Huwayjah"; Carpenter interview, 2 April 2008; SPC Joseph F. Herndon II was also struck in the chest by the RPG round, but was protected by his body armor. Despite two broken ribs, Herndon refused to be evacuated and stayed with his unit until the end of the action, receiving a Purple Heart. He received a second Purple Heart on 25 June 2004 and was killed in action in Hawijah on 29 July 2004. Herndon was the first Army victim of an expert enemy marksman nicknamed the "Hawijah sniper," who killed or wounded several other soldiers and contractors in Hawijah between 2004 and 2006. Herndon was the only KIA in the 1-27 IN in Hawijah during its one-year tour in the city and the first US soldier to die in the city during OIF. See Gregg K. Kakesako, "Comrades Eulogize Schofield Soldier," *Honolulu Star-Bulletin*, 3 August 2004, online at http://starbulletin.com/2004/ 08/03/news/index4.html, accessed on 3 April 2008.

30. Carpenter, "The Battle of Huwayjah."

31. Carpenter, "The Battle of Huwayjah"; Carpenter interview, 2 April 2008.

32. Carpenter interview, 2 April 2008.

33. Carpenter, "The Battle of Huwayjah."

34. Carpenter interview, 2 April 2008.

35. Carpenter interview, 26 March 2008; Staff SGT Samuel Bendet, "Photos: 'Operation Lion Victory' Celebrates Security Gains in Hawijah." Black Anthem Military News, 15 February 2008, online at http://www.blackanthem. com/News/iraqi-freedom/Photos-Operation-Lion-Victory-Celebrates-Security-Gains-in-Hawijah14572.shtml, accessed on 2 April 2008. The 2d Brigade was later redesignated as the 15th Brigade.

36. Bendet. In subsequent US troop rotations, Hawijah became a major battleground between US and later ISF units and insurgents. In early 2008, during the Baghdad surge operation, the Sunni Arab inhabitants of the Hawijah area finally and definitively turned against the insurgents, joining with the ISF through the formation of a 6,000-member Neighborhood Watch Association.

The following US forces were stationed at FOB McHenry from 2003 until 2008:

Unit	Date
1-12 IN (Mech) attached to the 173d Airborne Bde, 4th ID	2003-2004
1-27 IN, 2d Bde, 25th ID (under 1st ID)	2004-2005
1-163 IN (Mech) (MTARNG), 116th CAV Bde	2005
1-327 IN, 1st Bde, 101st Airborne Div	2005-2006
2-27 IN, 3d Bde, 25th ID	2006-2007
1-87 IN, 1st Bde, 10th Mountain Div	2007-2008

Task Force 1-26 Infantry
The Easter Sunday Battle of Samarra
April 2004

by

Matt M. Matthews

In July 2003, after the close of major combat operations related to Operation IRAQI FREEDOM, Task Force 1st Battalion, 66th Armor (TF 1-66 AR), 4th Infantry Division (4ID), constructed a forward operating base (FOB) west of Samarra, Iraq. The city, located on the east bank of the Tigris River in Salah Ad Din Province, was inhabited by approximately 200,000 people. Although the population of Samarra was predominately Sunni Arab, its celebrated Golden Mosque, containing the bodies of the Tenth and Eleventh Imams, made the city a sacred site for Shiite Muslims. With the arrival of 4th ID, the area quickly became a hotbed of insurgent activity. In the course of several months, the insurgents succeeded in driving a newly created Iraqi Civil Defense Corps (ICDC) battalion and the Iraqi National Police (INP) out of Samarra. In December 2003, the 4th ID struck back, launching Operation IVY BLIZZARD with the objective of destroying the enemy in Samarra, and restoring control of the city to the ICDC and INP. Unfortunately, insurgent leaders managed to flee the city before the attack. By February 2004, these leaders infiltrated back into the city, and renewed their assaults on the city government and coalition forces.[1]

In March 2004, the 1st Infantry Division (1ID) commanded by MG John S. Batiste, relieved the 4th ID in central Iraq. In Samarra TF 1st Battalion, 26th Infantry (TF 1-26 IN), commanded by LTC Kirk Allen, replaced TF 1-66. Allen's Task Force was part of the 2d Brigade Combat Team; (2 BCT), 1st ID, led by COL Randal Dragon. During this rotational shift, the situation in Samarra remained troublesome. 2 BCT operations officer (S-3), MAJ John Casper, summarized things as follows:

> Prior to the RIP (relief in place), 4th ID had conducted a major brigade operation in and around Samarra with the purpose of rooting out the insurgency that was already growing there, and that operation was just finishing up prior to the Rip. Again, the purpose of their operation was to try and collect all the targets they had been working over the last nine months there and try to kill or capture all those targets prior to us assuming that battlespace. The major effect of their operation was that they didn't actually kill or capture many of their targets but they did drive them into hiding in town. And some of their high-value targets (HVTs) did

19

leave town, only to return later. The forward operating base (FOB) we were on was called Brassfield-Mora and it was located along Main Supply Route or MSR TAMPA. It was a good location to monitor the MSR but a poor location to monitor Samarra, which was the main effort of the task force. It was about eight kilometers outside of town and on the opposite side of the Tigris River. That was a major challenge for us because we only had one way in and one way out of town.[2]

Allen's Task Force contained three company-sized maneuver elements. Team Alpha, commanded by CPT Benjamin Marlin, consisted of two Bradley platoons and a platoon of M1114 Up-Armored HMMWVs. CPT William Rockefeller led Team Bravo, consisting of two Bradley platoons and a platoon of four M1A1 Abrams tanks. A Vermont State Police trooper in civilian life, 1LT George Rodriguez, commanded Allen's third company, C Company, 2-108th Infantry, New York Army National Guard. Rodriguez's three platoons of air assault infantry were attached to Allen's heavy task force. Lacking their own organic vehicles, the New York Guardsmen were equipped with 5-ton trucks and a few HMMWVs with added armor. Many of the men in Charlie Company called their open top 5-ton trucks "RPG magnets."[3] One soldier believed "it was only a matter of time before we were hit, and we knew it."[4] Another Guardsman remarked, "You've got to be an idiot not to be able to hit it with an RPG."[5] Although Rodriguez and his men were able to secure armored platting for the sides of the 5-tons, the soldiers remained extremely vulnerable.

As TF 1-26 IN settled into FOB Brassfield-Mora, its major focus centered on "offensive operations to defeat anti-coalition forces, [and to] build credibility in transitioning for Iraqi self-governance, and ensure the secure and stable environment for all forces."[6] Allen stipulated in his commander's intent [that] "decisive to this effort is the maintenance of a dedicated and highly professional Iraqi Defense Corps (ICDC) battalion that is closely integrated with the police force in the protection of the local citizenry and government from hostile elements."[7]

At first, TF 1-26 IN made huge strides in carrying out the commander's objectives. "We had what we called the Samarra working group," Casper noted. "The Samarra working group was organized by our executive officer, MAJ Jeff Church, and it brought together all the key leaders that we thought were part of the city's governing council and their protective services."[8]

However, as the major Shiite holidays of Al Arba'eeniya Al Husseiniya and Ashura approached in April 2004, the security situation in Samarra began to deteriorate as the local Iraqi forces fell apart. Casper recalled:

For about the first 12 hours of this festival, around 5 to 6 April, the Iraqi Security Forces (ISF) did a fantastic job of setting up all their blocking positions, crowd control and security. Then an insurgent group attacked them, and once the first blocking position was attacked they melted away and that led to the entire security posture falling apart. The police melted away first, which left just the [ICDC] in place, and then they quickly melted away also. When I say "melted away," I mean they basically disappeared, except for about a third of the unit, which stood its ground. The rest of them disappeared and some never came back to work. They basically abandoned their post and left. The town had a security situation immediately following that. While they were securing the inner portions of the town, we were using our coalition forces to secure the outside of town.[9]

On 5 and 6 April, Team Bravo and Charlie Company began targeted operations in the city in an effort to regain some control from the insurgents. 1LT Rodriguez recalled there were "reports of police officers being killed and it was basically a free-for-all going on in Samarra."[10] Unfortunately, TF 1-26 did not have the manpower to restore order to the entire city. "There was still a security vacuum in town because the size of the town and the amount of troops we had did not correlate," Casper stated.[11] "We could not be in every section of the town at all times. We could surge with forces we had and cover about half the town for 24 hours, but we couldn't cover all of it. Every time we would move into a new section of town, the insurgents could melt into the local populace or they could move out of town into the farmlands if they could get outside our cordon."[12]

Samarra is on the east bank of the Tigris River. For the conduct of operations, the Americans had divided the city proper into twelve numbered sectors (see Map 3). Each sector was further divided into a number of zones which were given alphabetic designations. In addition to the sectors and zones, all the major routes through the city were given codenames. East-west roads were designated after NBA basketball teams. Route HEAT demarked the southernmost east-west street in Samarra. For north-south routes, the soldiers used the existing Iraqi street names. In this case the streets were numbered from west to east, with 60th Street being the road on the far east of the city. FOB Brassfield-Mora was located along Iraqi Highway 1, called by the Americans Main Supply Route (MSR) TAMPA, on the west side of the Tigris River several miles to the northwest of Samarra. The direct route from the FOB to the city crossed the Tigris over a large dam.

On the morning of 11 April, CPT Rockefeller's Team Bravo was assigned a cordon and search mission in the southwestern part of the city, a location identified on their map graphics as Zone 10 Oscar. Charlie Company, which had been occupying a tactical assembly area (TAA) and manning a TCP (traffic control point) southeast of Samarra, would support Bravo's operation by establishing a blocking position at the intersection of Route JAZZ and 20th Street. This location was several blocks west of Zone 10 Oscar. Having recently discovered an enemy cache of ammunition at his current location, Charlie commander Rodriguez had to leave behind his 3d Platoon and half of his 1st Platoon at the TAA to deal with the material.

Meanwhile, Team Alpha was assigned security duty at FOB Brassfield-Mora. During the execution of the operation, the battalion commander, LTC Allen, drove to FOB Dagger in Tikrit to meet with his brigade commander, COL Dragon. In Allen's absence, the battalion operations officer (S-3), MAJ John Casper, would be in charge of the operation. At that time, the only American soldiers in Samarra were a mortar section and quick reaction force (QRF) from the 10th Special Forces Group's Operational Detachment Alpha (ODA) 063. These Special Forces soldiers were located in a building known as the ODA house, which was situated in a western sector of the city.[13]

Late in the afternoon Team Bravo, with two mechanized infantry platoons of M2A2 ODS (the model originally developed for use in Operation DESERT STORM) Bradleys, and one platoon of M1A1 Abrams tanks, moved out of FOB Brassfield-Mora and headed east toward Samarra. The TF 1-26 Tactical Command Post (TAC), which consisted of operations officer (S-3) MAJ John Casper in his M2A2 ODS Bradley and operations SGM Ronald Pruyt in his M1114 HMMWV, followed Team Bravo. Two HMMWVs from the battalion scout platoon provided security for the TAC. As the units crossed the dam bridge into Samarra and headed toward Zone 10 Oscar, Team Bravo and the TAC noticed curious behavior on the part of the inhabitants. "Occasionally, when we'd enter town," Pruyt recalled, "we were met with kids waving at us; adults might not wave at us but they acknowledged they had seen us. This time when we rolled into town, shops started closing down. People were locking up and getting their kids off the streets. We noticed that right away and thought something was going on."[14] As Team Bravo and the TAC moved into the designated zone of operations, and Bravo began the search mission, the TAC sent out an urgent radio message to all elements, warning everyone to "be ready."[15]

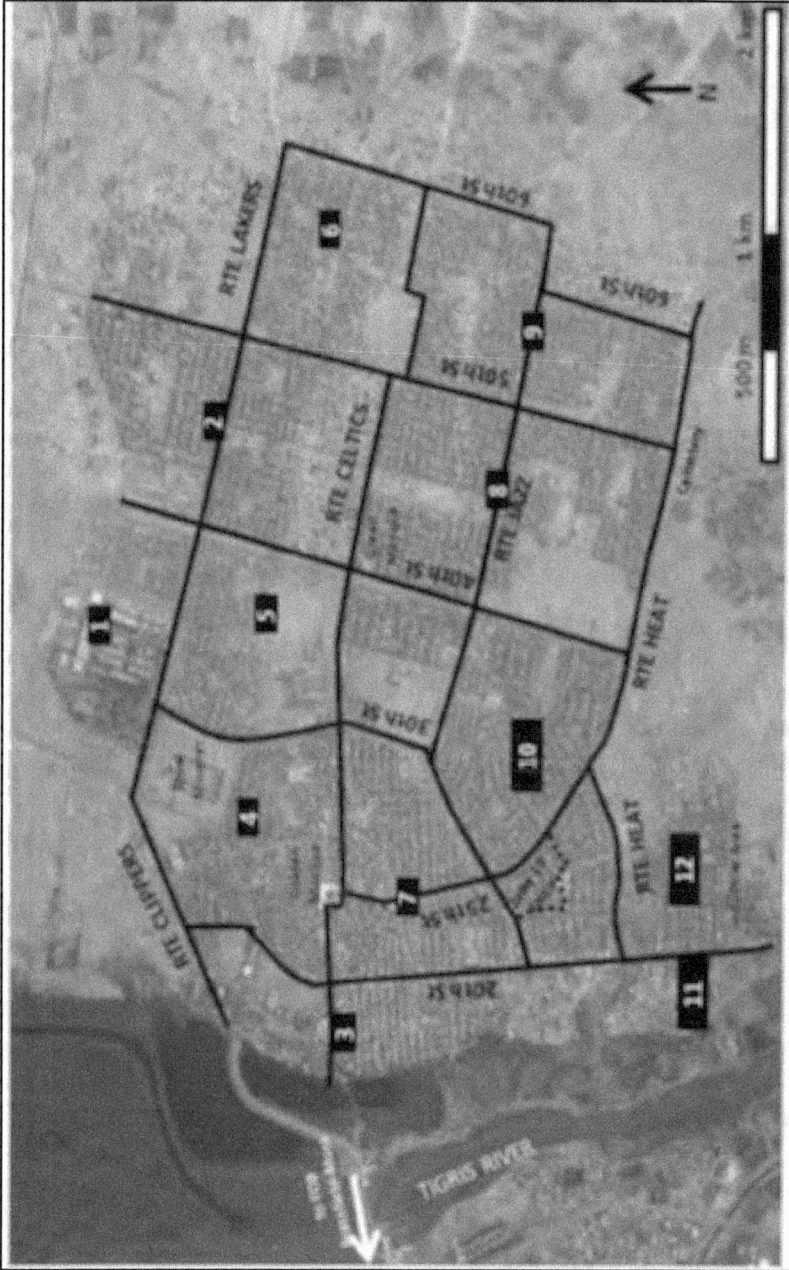

Map 3. Samarra, 2004.

23

At roughly the same time, starting from the TAA located in the opposite direction from Samarra than the FOB, Rodriguez's Charlie Company, consisting of 2d Platoon and half of 1st Platoon, turned onto Route HEAT at the southwestern corner of the city and headed west toward their blocking position at the intersection of Route JAZZ and 20th Street. Rodriguez led the way in his M966 HMMWV, which mounted a MK-19 grenade launcher. Following Rodriguez was another M966 armed with a M240B machine gun, and two 5-ton trucks, each mounting M240Bs and carrying about 13 or 14 infantrymen in their beds. Bringing up the rear were two additional M966s equipped with M240B machine guns, a total force of six vehicles. As the convoy moved west the soldiers riding in the back of the open top 5-tons scanned the rooftops for any sign of trouble. They immediately noticed the same odd lack of civilian presence Bravo had noted. From his perch in the back of one of the 5-tons, SPC Robert Hemsing remembered thinking, "Hey. Hold up. There's nobody outside. That little girl's running to her house. That car just turned around and went backwards down the street. Something's going on."[16]

Five minutes later, near the intersection of Route HEAT and 60th Street, at the western limit of Samarra, mortar rounds began to fall close to the convoy. As the first mortar round exploded, an IED (improvised explosive device) detonated next to the second 5-ton truck, destroying one of the tires on the middle axle of the vehicle. Within seconds a second IED exploded, rocking the convoy but doing no damage. Suddenly, enemy small arms fire exploded from the rooftops and alleyways north of the convoy, while insurgent machine-gun fire from a cemetery south of Charlie Company peppered the line of vehicles. Rodriguez and his men were in the midst of a well-orchestrated ambush. When the driver of the 5-ton truck in which Hemsing was riding pulled the vehicle next to a building to its right in order to gain cover, a rocket propelled grenade (RPG) slammed into the vehicle's side, but failed to penetrate the armor siding. However, almost immediately an insurgent appeared on the rooftop of the adjacent building and fired an RPG directly down into the bed of the truck. The explosion instantly killed 21-year-old PFC Nathan P. Brown as his body absorbed the brunt of the impact. "It turned everything yellow and green," SSG Troy Mechanick recalled.[17] The blast broke his left arm in four places and nearly severed the middle finger on his right hand. Jagged shards of metal also tore into Hemsing's legs, and severed three fingers on one hand and nearly severed one finger on the other. Also wounded were SPCs Timothy Durie, Mark Nellis, Matthew Arnold, and Chad Byrne. Durie was knocked out of the gun turret. Despite his wounds, he managed to crawl back into the gunner position and return fire with the M240B machine gun. From the truck bed, the other soldiers managed to return fire as well. Caught in a hail of gunfire, the insurgent who had fired the RPG was quickly killed, his body riddled with bullets.[18]

From the driver's side of the vehicle, SPC Timmy Haag fired his SAW (squad automatic weapon) at the insurgents in the cemetery to the left, killing two and perhaps three of them. Working their way past their wounded comrades, Haag and SPC James MacDonald jumped off the back end of the truck. "For some reason it made sense for me just to shoot the area where I was looking at," Haag recalled.[19] Under a hail of gunfire, Haag and MacDonald ran west up the street (Route HEAT) in a desperate attempt to find Rodriguez and inform him of the situation. Rushing past alleyways filled with insurgents firing AK-47s and RPGs, Haag fired back, inflicting considerable damage on the enemy. Both men made it to the front of the convoy uninjured.

When the ambush began, Rodriguez was in his up-armored HMMWV at the head of the column. "For about the first minute there was a lot of chaos, and after about 30 seconds, the soldiers started dismounting out of the 5-tons," he remembered.[20] "At this time, I received word that we had one KIA and five or six wounded."[21] By now, all the uninjured soldiers from Charlie Company had dismounted their trucks and were firing back. "When we dismounted," Rodriguez remembered, "it seemed like the insurgents were really taken by surprise and didn't know what to do."[22] Unable to get a good view of the situation from inside his vehicle, Rodriguez leaped out of the HMMWV as bullets skipped across the street and whizzed past his head. The first vehicles of the convoy had travelled beyond the kill zone of the insurgent ambush. "From the angle we were at, we could actually see into the side of the ambush positions where they were laying down," he recalled. "I had a MK-19 on my vehicle so I pointed out the targets and my gunner started engaging them with the MK-19 for about 30 seconds. He fired a whole box of MK-19 rounds into that ambush position."[23] In short order, this raking fire managed to suppress the enemy fire coming from the cemetery.

After linking up with Rodriguez, Haag and MacDonald ran back to their truck. As they scrambled up the ladder into the back of the vehicle, Haag unleashed a torrent of fire from his SAW at the enemy along the rooftops. Just as he moved to this new position in the truck bed, an RPG round bounced off the road precisely where Haag had been standing only a second before. Out of ammo for his SAW, he grabbed the nearest available weapon and continued to fire back as the truck began slowly lurching forward.[24]

Rodriguez now decided to transport his casualties to the Special Forces medics at the ODA house as quickly as possible. Accordingly, he moved the 5-ton with the wounded in the bed, along with his own vehicle and two other M966s away from the ambush site to the intersection of HEAT and 25th Street. After reorganizing and sorting out the wounded at an impromptu casualty collection point, Rodriguez sent the 5-ton, with two HMMWVs to provide security, off to the ODA house. The small convoy was guided by a Blue Force Tracker digital navigation system to the secret SF location. Jumping into his vehicle, Rodriguez returned to the ambush site. As he rolled into the site, his MK-19 gunner fired upon insurgents positioned on the rooftops to the north. Soon, the remaining Charlie Company dismounted troops, consisting of approximately14 men, had pushed the insurgents back down the alleyways and away from Route HEAT. As Rodriguez and his men returned fire, enemy mortar rounds continued to explode around them, and they found themselves taking fire from a mosque at the intersection of HEAT and 50th Street.[25]

When Team Bravo received word of Charlie Company's predicament, Rockefeller's men were conducting their cordon and search. Despite the odd behavior of the local population, Team Bravo had made no enemy contact so far. Rockefeller suspended his house-by-house search and had his men remount their vehicles. However, communications difficulties hindered the ability of Team Bravo to reinforce Charlie Company at the ambush site. "For me, the hardest part of the initial part of that battle was trying to figure out where he was," the Team Bravo commander remembered.[26] "That caused a lot of confusion with my company when I was told to go down and help him out. I never caught him on the Blue Force Tracker."[27] Rockefeller recalled:

> He sent me a grid, which I thought was down by 40th Street and HEAT, which was actually very close to where we were… Anyway, we started to get everybody back in the vehicles. We're going to move over there and assist Charlie Company and whatever contact they were in, but I really didn't know how significant the contact was at that point. I asked him again where the contact was and I got a grid from right in the middle of the industrial area [Sector12]. At that point I was completely turned around. I was moving the company down 25th Street moving towards 40th and HEAT. We're all moving easterly and then I get a grid that says they're in a different location, right in the middle of the industrial area, so at that point I was going the wrong way.[28]

Confused by the conflicting grid coordinates, Rockefeller ordered his company to halt and scan the area in an attempt to locate Charlie Company. "No one is seeing anything at this point," the commander stated:

> I made the decision to start turning people around to move to the industrial area and that's when somebody sees something up at the mosque on 50th and HEAT. We then see a bunch of Charlie Company vehicles moving through our position. Now we know they aren't down in the industrial area; they're on HEAT to the east. At that point, half my company is turned around heading towards the industrial area and the other half is facing the right direction. I decided to take who was facing in the right direction and take them down to HEAT and 50th and see what was going on down there.[29]

As Team Bravo began its move, its members observed the two Charlie Company HMMWVs and the damaged 5-ton truck with the wounded heading north on 20th Street. As the men in Team Bravo watched, an IED exploded next to the cargo truck, ripping out the center right tire. Immediately, the Charlie Company soldiers manning the M240Bs in the M966s fired at the man who had detonated the IED, killing him and two of his compatriots as the convoy continued moving speedily northwards toward the ODA house.[30]

As the Charlie Company vehicles drove out of sight, the TAC group followed several vehicles from Team Bravo as it headed east to link up with the rest of Rodriguez's company. "So, I received the call that they had been hit and were moving out," SGM Pruyt remembered:

> There was some confusion as to where they were due to the heat and confusion of battle. We started moving towards where we know they're going to be at to help secure the area. As we were making a turn, some are moving and some are stopped, but everybody is ready and on high alert status. There were kids who came out on the street and somebody threw some firecrackers. It sounded like a whole pack of firecrackers had been lit. I know it wasn't AK47 rounds…I just know there were kids on the streets with firecrackers going off and that set everybody on edge a little bit. We know we have an element in contact and then we have this stuff going on. It was quite surreal.[31]

During the move toward Charlie Company, Team Bravo and the TAC, too, came under insurgent fire. "We were traveling behind the S-3's Bradley," Pruyt stated. "He pulls off to the side and starts receiving some fire, so he fired his Bradley to the south. That's when he had asked Lieutenant Rodriquez, who we hadn't linked up with yet, to pop purple smoke so we could find out where he was to go and help secure him—but we couldn't see the smoke."[32] Apparently, Rodriguez was missing some of his map graphics and was unable to give the TAC or Team Bravo his exact location. "At that point we were in contact with battalion, and Bravo Company was moving toward us," Rodriguez recalled. "There was some confusion at first on where we exactly were. We had an older map."[33]

As the purple smoke dissipated, Rodriquez popped a canister of red smoke. Within a few minutes, members of the TAC saw the red smoke drifting skyward and continued its move toward Rodriguez and his men. As soon as Rodriquez was informed that his location had been identified, he began pulling his men out of the ambush site and moving them west on Route HEAT in an effort to link up with Team Bravo. "We had to dismount from the vehicles and secure the road intersections and multiple alleyways running into the main road," he stated.[34] "We secured this, returned fire until the vehicles were past the intersection, and then we moved up to the next intersection…We kept doing this until we reached Bravo Company."[35]

Enemy mortar fire continued to explode around them as they moved. Rodriquez could see the insurgents firing the mortars off to his southwest, but lacked a weapons system capable of hitting them. When Rodriquez called for an artillery strike on the enemy mortar positions, his request was denied. "They simply didn't want to fire that close to the city," he later explained.[36]

At this point, and while still under heavy fire from the enemy, Rodriquez and the remainder of his company headed off to the ODA house to check on their wounded comrades. As he drove west, Rodriquez radioed his 3d Platoon and first sergeant, who were still in the TAA south of the city. "I told them to remain south of the city until air [support] arrived. Air would guide them around the city and we could link up at the ODA house," he stated.[37] Ten minutes after arriving at the ODA house an ambulance arrived from FOB Brassfield-Mora. "They loaded all the wounded into the FLA [Front Line Ambulance] and were taken back to Brassfield-Mora and airlifted out of there," Rodriguez recalled.[38]

By the time Rockefeller arrived at 50th and HEAT with his headquarters element and 3d Platoon, enemy fire had ceased. "There was no contact at that point," he recalled. "I didn't see it and didn't hear it, but it was obvious that something was happening because there was debris from vehicles and spent shell casings on the ground."[39] The Team Bravo commander now began to assess the current situation. His unit was spread out along Route HEAT. The 2d Platoon was at the intersection of 40th and HEAT, the tank platoon at 25th and HEAT, and his headquarters and 3d Platoon at 50th and HEAT. Rockefeller decided to move through the city along the main north-south streets up to Route LAKERS, the east-west street that marked the northern edge of the built-up area. Once at LAKERS, all elements would move to the intersection of that route and Route CLIPPERS in the northwestern corner of the city, an intersection marked by the large spiral minaret, a Samarra landmark that was impossible to miss. Rockefeller gave his intent to his subordinate leaders: "I told them that if we got to LAKERS, we'd all rally up at Route CLIPPERS and LAKERS in front of the minaret and figure out what we're going to do from there."[40]

1LT Jacob White's 3d Platoon, followed by Rockefeller, the Team Bravo headquarters elements, and the battalion TAC immediately started north on 50th Street. As the vehicles moved up the street, the entire element came under heavy small arms and RPG fire. One RPG ripped into White's Bradley, penetrating the rear of his TOW launcher and exploding. Fortunately, no one inside the Bradley was injured. [41] As the armored vehicles continued to move north, the company headquarters element, consisting of four up-armored HMMWVs and a 5-ton cargo truck, as well as the two vehicles of the TAC, began to fall behind. SGM Pruyt explained what happened next:

> There are people up on the roofs, and more than what we could fight through at that point. So we engaged and then turned around. I think I was driving behind a tank. I saw two or three RPG rounds fly between me and the tank and we were no more than 10 to 15 meters apart from each other. There were guys popping around corners, firing and popping back in the houses. I had my window down in the 1114 and was firing at them. My 240 gunner was up top and was engaging targets as well. So we turned around and came back out because one of the other Bravo Company 5-tons had been hit by an RPG that skipped down the road and went between the first sergeant [1SG Noel Salinas] and another guy. The RPG damaged the hub and tires and wounded a soldier. That's when one of Bravo Company's master gunners, SFC Chris Borneman, went out and evacuated the soldier, and he was getting shot at the whole time, but he pulled him out [and] brought him over to a HMMWV.[42]

As the Team Bravo headquarters element and the TAC fought desperately to fend off the enemy, Rockefeller and his 3d Platoon continued on and arrived at the rally point at the intersection of Route LAKERS and CLIPPERS. As they pulled into the intersection they were quickly joined by 1LT Tyrone Jones' 1st Platoon of four Abrams tanks. Jones had made his way up 30th Street without any enemy contact.[43] While the 2d Platoon, moving down 40th Street, had not yet arrived, Rockefeller noticed that the rear part of his own convoy, his headquarters element and the TAC were missing:

> I realized that my headquarters section was strung out. Apparently they made contact but I never got a radio call that said they made contact. They had been right behind me. Somehow, something happened to one of the vehicles. They were still at 50th and HEAT, and they were in contact, but I didn't know that until I got up to LAKERS with 3rd Platoon.[44]

While this force had turned back to the south, Rockefeller's 2d Platoon was also in trouble. Having turned north up 40th Street, 1LT Michael Gunther's 2d Platoon also came under heavy RPG and small arms fire. To further complicate the situation, Gunther's platoon consisted of only three Bradleys. And the platoon leader's Bradley had lost its integrated sight unit (ISU), forcing Gunther to fight exposed from the turret. Additionally, he was having communications difficulties. He could not reach Rockefeller on the radio. At the corner of 40th and CELTICS, midway across the city, the 2d Platoon entered a hornet's nest as the enemy fired a torrent of RPGs at the American vehicles. Much of the fire was coming from the Green Mosque located in the southeast corner of the intersection. During the heated exchange, Gunther's men killed 11 insurgents.

Meanwhile, slightly to the east, the Bravo Team headquarters elements and the TAC remained locked in combat and were forced to call for help over the company radio net. SFC William Baggett, the 2d Platoon sergeant, responded quickly. With Gunther's approval, Baggett broke off from the rest of the platoon and blasted his way southeast to 50th and HEAT. The bold move allowed 1SG Salinas to momentarily break contact and reorganize his force. Assembling back where they started at the intersection of 50th and HEAT, Baggett, the headquarters element, and the TAC established a hasty defensive perimeter. Firing in all directions, this force managed to kill an additional 10 insurgents.[45]

Rockefeller, at the designated rendezvous point at the intersection of Routes CLIPPERS and LAKERS, knew nothing of these events. He faced a serious dilemma. With his 2d Platoon missing, and lacking information on the whereabouts of his headquarters section and the TAC, Rockefeller had to act quickly:

> The tanks showed up and I was calling 2d Platoon wondering what their status was. Then I called back to the First Sergeant to get his status and I'm not getting any response. I left 3d Platoon to secure that intersection because that was my exit out of the city, and it was a horrible place for IEDs along that route. They [3d Platoon] were sitting right across from the spiral minaret and they're looking down CLIPPERS to make sure no IEDs are being emplaced so, if we have any casualties, I can get those guys out of there unhindered...I could not get ahold of anybody in 2d Platoon and half of my headquarters section was still in contact so, I knew we had to move. I took my vehicle and four tanks, [and] went to 40th Street, and we came down 40th Street looking for 2d Platoon. We found them down there and they were in contact.[46]

Within minutes, Rockefeller's Bradley and Jones' tanks arrived at 40th and CELTICS, linking up with Gunther's remaining two Bradleys. At the same time, two AH-64 Apache helicopters from the 1st Battalion, 1st Aviation Regiment, arrived overhead. As they hovered nearby, an RPG fired from the Green Mosque hit the tail rotor of one of the aircraft, forcing both AH-64s to return to FOB Speicher at the Tikrit airfield.[47]

As Rockefeller's tanks and Bradleys continued to work their way south to 40th and HEAT, their combined firepower began to rapidly reduce the number of insurgents on the street. "There were some guys down there," Rockefeller recalled. "Once we started returning fire, though, that started to melt away."[48] Gunther immediately informed Rockefeller that he had sent one of his Bradleys to assist the headquarters element and the TAC on 50th and HEAT. Wasting no time, the Team Bravo commander ordered his men to head east down Route HEAT to join up with the forces at 50th and HEAT.[49]

The Team Bravo vehicles roared into the intersection at 50th and HEAT, linking up with the missing headquarters section and the TAC. As the four tanks, two Bradleys and Rockefeller's HMMWV pulled into the intersection, the fire from the insurgents quickly diminished. "At that point," according to Rockefeller, "we had about two-and-a-half platoons of combat power down there and the contact kind of melted away again."[50] Concerned about repairing the damaged 5-ton truck in such proximity to the buildings on the north side of Route HEAT, the Team

Bravo Commander moved everyone 400 meters south of Route HEAT and hastily set up a defensive perimeter at a position south of the cemetery where Rodriguez had made his first contact earlier.[51]

Just as the perimeter was being established, the insurgents once again opened fire from the buildings north of Route HEAT. "We moved out just far enough to set up a perimeter and work on the [5-ton] tire," Rockefeller remembered. "At that point though, we started taking RPGs. It was hard for me to ascertain where the contact was coming from. Some of it was coming from the area around the Green Mosque and some of it was actually coming from the garbage heaps south of the city."[52] Standing outside his M1114, SGM Pruyt watched in amazement as an RPG sailed over his head:

> We set up a perimeter while we get this 5-ton to where it can roll on its own. While we're doing that, we start receiving fire from the city. I'm looking over there, pulling security outside of my 1114, and making sure other people are pulling security too. The RPGs start flying over our heads, probably about five meters over my head, and landed on a berm about 20 meters behind me. My gunner starts engaging and returning fire on where this fire came from. While we were there in the middle of consolidating, reorganizing, and getting this vehicle running, the guys had mentioned that they thought they were receiving fire from one of the mosques. It was then confirmed; we had guys looking through binoculars who saw people moving around…There were guys up there firing AK47s and RPGs at us.[53]

Rockefeller promptly ordered his men to silence the enemy fire coming from the Green Mosque. SFC Manuel Cantiga responded immediately, firing nine 120-mm tank main gun rounds into the mosque. As the rounds ripped huge holes through the structure, the enemy fire slackened, then stopped.[54]

With the insurgent fire abated, Rockefeller made the decision to move the entire force back to the north side of Samarra and link up with his 3d Platoon, which was still at the intersection of Routes CLIPPERS and LAKERS. In order to minimize enemy contact, the Team Bravo commander decided to move around the east side of the city. Since the damaged 5-ton was still not running properly, he opted to have it towed. "We decided that rather than try to fight through the city with this towed vehicle, we'll skirt around the outside of the city and link up with our other platoon," he recalled.[55] Before they could move out, someone reminded Rockefeller that Charlie Company's 3d Platoon, commanded by 2LT Joseph Merrill, was still manning the TAA farther south of the city. Following Rodriguez' instructions, Merrill had been waiting for air support to help guide his platoon back through Samarra. At last, two OH-58D Kiowa Warrior helicopters arrived on station and provided cover for the 3d Platoon to move to Team Bravo's location. With the entire force assembled, and the OH-58Ds overhead in support, Rockefeller moved the entire command on a two-kilometer detour around the east side of the city. At 1800, Rockefeller linked up with his 3d Platoon about one kilometer north of Samarra.[56]

Finished with their escort mission, the OH-58Ds started back south over the city. They were soon met with a heavy barrage of small arms fire which wounded one of the pilots, forcing the aircraft to return to Rockefeller's location. The Team Bravo Commander sent the wounded pilot and his own wounded soldier back to the ODA house, escorted by Charlie Company's 3d Platoon. Once at the ODA house, Merrill linked up with his commander, 1LT Rodriguez, and the rest of Charlie Company. "We were just staging at the ODA house waiting for any follow-on missions when we got the word that 3rd Platoon was moving towards the ODA house," Rodriguez stated.[57] "We linked up with them and moved back to the FOB."[58] Setting up a defensive perimeter, Rockefeller waited for orders from his task force commander, LTC Kirk Allen. When the attack on Charlie Company began at 1605, Allen was in a conference with the brigade commander, COL Dragon, at FOB Dagger. Allen remarked:

> Somewhere towards the end of the meeting. somebody came in and said that something was going down in Samarra. I went to the brigade command center there and made a phone call. I found out 2-108 was ambushed and there were casualties. At that point I turned to the brigade commander, told him I was leaving, and that we had a firefight underway.[59]

Racing back to FOB Brassfield-Mora, Allen mounted his command Bradley, assembled the battalion scout platoon and headed east with that platoon to Samarra.

As Rodriguez and his company sped west toward FOB Brassfield-Mora, they passed Allen's Bradley, an M1114 commanded by the battalion personnel officer (S-1), and five M1025 Scout HMMVVVs from the battalion scout platoon, all headed east into the city. "My element moved to the north side of the city and the S-3 was already positioned with Team Bravo north of the city," Allen recalled.[60] After crossing the Tigris bridge,

Allen and his patrol linked up with Team Bravo and secured the intersection at Route CLIPPERS and LAKERS. With four tanks and 10 Bradleys at his disposal, the task force commander was anxious to move back into the city and regain contact with the insurgents. "The battalion commander's on station now," Pruyt stated, "so they wanted us to go back into town pushing from the north down to the south and go to the vicinity of the Green Mosque."[61] Allen decided to wait until dark to launch the attack so that his troops could take advantage of their night vision capabilities. While they waited for the sun to go down, the TAC swung into action. Casper remembered:

> There were some other things we started doing at this point as well. We started to work non-lethal effects to the point where we gained contact with the town council leadership, told them what was going on and asked them to impose a curfew for everybody to go inside. They did it and it went out over the mosque speakers. They told everyone to go home and stay inside. They very effectively got a hold of the imam and put a call out over the net to cease the attacks and for everybody to get home and stay inside. That went very well and we stayed in an assembly area to the north while this was happening.[62]

The Americans also tried to make the local police chief and ING battalion more effective. The effort failed with the police but was more successful with the ING unit.

This group of about 80 who were very loyal to the Iraqi battalion commander stayed and never left their post. When this attack commenced, they were quick to come up on the net so we held them in reserve in case we needed them later.[63]

The division soon provided unmanned aerial vehicles (UAVs) and field artillery support to fire on the enemy hub at the mosque in the middle of the city. The arrival of this support took less than an hour.

At 2100 Team Bravo once again began moving south to engage the enemy. Rockefeller recalled what happened next:

> We decided we would come down 40th Street, which was [nicknamed] Power Line Road, because it had high tension power lines along the road. We were going to come down 40th and there was an area there that would allow me, if I wanted to, to get two platoons abreast. ... The street was wide enough and the houses weren't up to the street. They were about 100 meters off the street so we could get two platoons, if we had to, moving

abreast…We pushed the tanks down and got them on line as best as possible. … We were going to lead with the tanks and come down Power Line Road. … We crossed over LAKERS and there was no significant contact, but between CELTICS and LAKERS we started receiving mortar fire.[64]

The advancing company also began receiving incoming small arms fire from the area of the Green Mosque. The unit stopped to allow the 155-mm howitzer at FOB Brassfield-More to fire on the Mosque. The round landed 100 meters southwest of the building.

No one is sure why the round fired from the M109A6 Paladin 155-mm self-propelled howitzer missed the target. The impact of the explosion so close to their position however, caused the insurgents in the Green Mosque to stop firing. When Rockefeller requested that they reengage the target, battalion staff, fearing collateral damage in the city, denied his request.[65] While Team Bravo was moving south toward the Green Mosque, Allen and his combat vehicles attacked south down the parallel 30th Street to the west. As this element moved closer to 30th and CELTICS, Allen's gunner fired his 25-mm gun at two insurgents carrying RPG-7s, killing them instantly. On observing the scene, one of Allen's men found only "a hand, a leg, and a pool of blood next to the damaged RPG-7."[66]

At approximately 2200, Rockefeller maneuvered his team past the mosque and continued to move south toward Route JAZZ, the next major cross street. It was then he realized his vehicles were running extremely low on ammunition and fuel. "At this point" he recalled, "we were several hours into it. We were going black on ammo and fuel."[67] Team Bravo needed resupply that was only available at FOB Brassfield-Mora.

Allen now faced two critical decisions. Should he continue the action after resupplying Team Bravo? And if so, with what forces could they continue? A decision to call off the fight would be prudent. Team Bravo and Charlie Company had been under enemy fire for over six hours. Charlie Company had taken casualties. Both units had lost vehicles. The troops were fatigued. This was their first intense firefight since being deployed to Iraq. With one company guarding the FOB (Alpha) and another (Charlie) emotionally drained from the fierce firefight, Allen's ability to optimally mass forces was limited.[68]

However, Allen recognized there were advantages to continuing the action as well. If TF 1-26 IN left and did not return, the insurgents could consider that they had driven the Americans out of the city. And breaking contact could allow the insurgents time to regroup. Additionally, the earlier fights had helped to identify where in the city the bulk of the insurgents were. American efforts could concentrate from the start on the 50th Street area between JAZZ and HEAT. The Americans also had a definite advantage in a nocturnal battle with their night vision equipment. Most importantly, Allen's troops had the initiative. Continuing the action would allow the Americans to retain this advantage.

For a return to battle, Allen had to look at what forces were available to him. He had three maneuver elements. Team Alpha was guarding the FOB, a vital mission. And Alpha had not yet experienced a firefight of the intensity that was expected. Team Bravo was tired but, once resupplied, would be otherwise in good shape. Charlie Company, too, was exhausted, had suffered some casualties and its 5-ton trucks could prove to be particularly vulnerable in a night fight in a city.

Allen decided to renew the action. Casper remembered:

The battalion commander decided to return to the FOB for a quick refit, to brief Alpha Company, and bring them into the mission also. We withdrew to our FOB, which is another reason why our FOB was not ideally located. Had it been located right in town, we wouldn't have had to break contact with the enemy; but since it was located so far away we had to withdraw. We did leave eyes on the town. ... While we were refitting, the battalion XO, the Headquarters and Headquarters Company (HHC) commander, and the support platoon leader did a fabulous job of getting things ready at the FOB.[69]

With such preparations, the troops quickly refueled and rearmed. While the soldiers ate, the battalion command group developed the plan for the continuation of the operation. Alpha company was released from FOB security duties to participate in the renewed effort.[70]

During this quick resupply operation, Alpha Company geared up and it was going to be Bravo and Alpha back into the city at that point. The center of gravity was along 50th Street between JAZZ and HEAT. We knew what was going on and we couldn't just let it lie at that point. We were seen rolling out of the city and we didn't want to present weakness, so we decided we'd go back in and spend the night in the city. If need be, we'd be there in the morning when the sun came up and they'd know we didn't run away.[71]

Allen assumed the risk and had HHC personnel relieve Alpha on FOB security detail. Teams Alpha and Bravo would lead the attack, with the TAC/Scout group augmenting them. The pause proved to be short. "From the time we rolled back onto the FOB to the time we rolled back out, it had to be less than 90 minutes," SGM Pruyt recalled.[72] "The commanders and staff came up with a real quick plan to go down, regain contact and destroy them. I rolled back out with the TAC with my guys. I changed some of my TAC guys out because I wanted other guys to have some experience and see what was going on."[73]

While the soldiers conducted their pre-combat checks and quickly devoured their Easter Sunday dinner, Allen met with his key officers in the tactical operations center (TOC). The battalion executive officer, MAJ Jeffrey Church, would control the fight from the TOC and coordinate the new mission with the brigade TOC. Allen's plan called for Team Bravo to cross the bridge and push rapidly east on CELTICS, establishing blocking positions at 50th and CELTICS, while Team Alpha moved east down Route HEAT, turning north at 50th and HEAT. Allen expected Team Alpha to drive the enemy into Team Bravo's blocking position.[74] Casper laterdescribed the disposition of the officers involved in the meeting:

> The mood was very positive. There was nobody there who did not want to go back in. There was anticipation that we would make contact. After being there for 45 days and mostly dealing with hit-and-run tactics, the commanders were upbeat and everybody was upbeat because it looked like they were going to stand and fight. We saw this as a good opportunity to fight them on their own ground but at the time of our choosing, which would be at night. So we saw this as a good opportunity to eliminate some of the insurgents in the area. I don't remember any exact words but I do remember the mood was generally upbeat and everybody was looking forward to going back in and rooting the insurgents out while they were still emboldened and thought they could fight us… Alpha and Bravo were going to move on parallel routes from the west side of town to the east side of town; that was where we had pinpointed enemy locations from the use of the UAV.[75]

Allen, Team Alpha, Team Bravo, and the TAC, accompanied by the scout platoon, left the FOB at 0100. "Almost immediately we started making contact," Pruyt remembered.[76] Traveling east on Route HEAT, Marlin's Team Alpha, following the plan, turned north at 50th Street and moved to the intersection of 50th and JAZZ, where they set up a security perimeter. As 2LT Peter Park's 2d Platoon dismounted from their Bradleys and began searching the alleys, his Bradleys and two M1114 HMMWVs from the 1st Platoon came under a withering barrage of RPG and small arms fire. Fortunately, his platoon remained unscathed, and managed to kill one enemy fighter with a 25-mm gun. While the 2d Platoon continued to spar with insurgents firing from rooftops and from behind vehicles, Marlin's 3d Platoon moved east on JAZZ. Turning south on 60th Street, the platoon's Bradleys were hit by multiple RPGs fired from rooftops and alleyways. Despite the pummeling, the 3d Platoon continued to kill insurgents.

Meanwhile, Rockefeller's Team Bravo crossed the bridge into Samarra, moving from Route CLIPPERS to LAKERS, turning south on 30th Street, and then east on CELTICS. At 40th and CELTICS, opposite the Green Mosque, the 3d Platoon dismounted, while the tank platoon continued on to 50th and CELTICS. Arriving at that intersection, the tanks were greeted by a volley of RPG rockets. One of the tanks fired its main gun at two insurgents in the street, killing both instantly. Shortly thereafter, a force of ICDC soldiers arrived at 40th and CELTICS to conduct a search of the grounds outside the Green Mosque. Allen and the TAC also took up a position near the Green Mosque. Elements of Team Alpha linked up with Team Bravo at 40th and CELTICS, at which time Team Alpha began clearing back south toward ROUTE JAZZ.

By 0400 the fighting had stopped. "Alpha and Bravo Companies went in, engaged, and quickly destroyed guys who were walking around with RPGs," Pruyt recalled. He added:

> They were coming up and trying to engage and I guess they thought we couldn't see them but our guys took care of them pretty quickly. I think the word spread pretty quickly throughout the AIF [Anti-Iraqi Forces] that, 'Hey, we should go home; we're getting spanked out here.' So contact died down pretty quickly and we pushed through our objectives, consolidated, reorganized and pulled out of the city. That was pretty much it for the Battle of Easter Sunday.[77]

Without doubt, Allen's bold night attack was highly successful. Casper was convinced that the enemy "felt they had an advantage over us after the ambush of Charlie Company…They were emboldened and their big mistake was that night, when we had thermal imagery and Bradleys and tanks and they didn't."[78] At 0400, Allen ordered his men back to the FOB, and by 0500 the entire force had returned. In the 15-hour fight, TF 1-26 killed approximately 45 insurgents while sustaining one KIA and seven wounded.[79]

Allen's battalion was successful in Samarra because he was able to coordinate the movements and actions of all of his subordinate elements while at the same time using his armored vehicles and night vision optics to their maximum advantage The operation was a classic example of the use of combined arms and the synchronization of combat, combat support, and combat support assets to defeat an insurgent force in a complex urban environment.

Notes

1. "Task Force 1-26 Infantry History: The Battle of Easter Sunday, 11-12 April 2004, Samarra, Iraq Operation Iraqi Freedom II," compiled by the staff of TF 1-26 Infantry, n.d., 1-2, (hereafter cited as TF 1-26 History); MG John R.S. Batiste and LTC Paul R. Daniels, "The Fight for Samarra: Full-Spectrum Operations in Modern Warfare," *Military Review* (May-June 2005): 14-15.

2. MAJ John Casper, interview by author, 30 August 2006, Fort Leavenworth.

3. Devlin Barrett, Associated Press Writer, Washington (AP) 12 May 2004; "TF 1-26 History," 2.

4. "TF 1-26 History," 2.

5. "TF 1-26 History," 2.

6. "TF 1-26 History," 1.

7. "TF 1-26 History," 1.

8. Casper interview.

9. Casper interview.

10. CPT George Rodriguez, interview by author, 31 August 2006, Fort Leavenworth.

11. Casper interview.

12. Casper interview.

13. Task Force 1-26 History, 2.

14. SGM Ron Pruyt, interview by author, 26 August 2006, Leavenworth; Task Force 1-26 History, 3-4; Rodriguez, interview.

15. Pruyt, interview; Task Force 1-26 History, 3-4; Rodriguez, interview.

16. Tom Brokaw, "*To War and Back: The Story of Seven Young Men*," MSNBC.com, online at http://www.msnbc.msn.com/id/10487620/page/2/print/1/ displaymode/1098, accessed 11 September 2006, 3; TF 1-26 History, 4.

17. Brokaw, *To War and Back*, 3.

18. CPT George Rodriguez, interview by author, 31 August 2006; Tom Brokaw, *To War and Back*, 3.

19. Michael Daly, "A Gutsy G.I. Rescues Sitting-Duck Platoon," *The New York Daily News*, 16 May 2004.

20. Rodriguez interview.

21. Rodriguez interview.

22. Rodriguez interview.

23. Rodriguez interview.

24. Michael Daly, "A Gutsy G.I."

25. Rodriguez interview.

26. CPT William Rockefeller, interview by author, 30 October 2006, Fort Leavenworth.

27. Rockefeller interview.

28. Rockefeller interview.

29. Rockefeller interview.

30. "TF 1-26 History," 6.

31. Pruyt interview.

32. Pruyt interview.

33. Rodriguez interview.

34. Rockefeller interview.

35. Interestingly, CPT Rockefeller reported he never saw Charlie Company. "I never saw Charlie. I saw a couple vehicles go by, but I never saw Charlie at all." Rockefeller interview.

36. Rodriguez interview.

37. Rodriguez interview.

38. Rodriguez interview.

39. Rockefeller interview.

40. Rockefeller interview.

41. "TF 1-26 History."

42. Pruyt interview.

43. "TF 1-26 History."

44. Rockefeller interview.

45. "TF 1-26 History."

46. Rockefeller interview.

47. "TF 1-26 History."

48. Rockefeller interview.

49. Rockefeller interview.

50. Rockefeller interview; "TF 1-26 History."

51. Rockefeller interview; "TF 1-26 History"; SGM Ron Pruyt thought they moved 300 meters south of the city.

52. Pruyt interview.

53. Pruyt interview.

54. Rockefeller interview; TF 1-26 History.

55. Rockefeller interview.

56. Rockefeller interview.

57. LTC Kirk Allen, interview by author, 31 August 2006; Rockefeller interview.

58. Allen interview; Rockefeller interview.

59. Allen interview; Rockefeller interview.

60. Rockefeller interview.

61. Pruyt interview.

62. Casper interview.

63. Casper interview.

64. Rockefeller interview.

65. Rockefeller interview.

66. "TF 1-26 History," 10.

67. Rockefeller interview.

68. Rockefeller interview.

69. Casper interview.

70. Casper interview.

71. Rockefeller interview.

72. Pruyt interview.

73. Pruyt interview.

74. "TF 1-26 History," 12.

75. Casper interview.

76. Pruyt interview; TF 1-26 History, 13-14.

77. Pruyt interview.

78. Casper interview.

79. "TF 1-26 History," 14.

Taking it to the Enemy: Offensive Counterinsurgency Operations

1st Battalion, 24th Infantry
Mosul 2004-2005

by

John J. McGrath

Terrorists, we are coming for you!
You cannot escape us; We hunt you by day,
We hunt you by night.
Do not run...You will only die tired.
-Poster in the Office of LTC Erik Kurilla, Commander, 1-24th Infantry[1]

Mosul is the third-largest city in Iraq and the capital of the northern province of Nineveh. The city has a mixed population of Sunni Arabs, Kurds and sizeable Christian and Turkmen minorities. Thus it represents all the ethnic challenges in a microcosm facing a post-Baathist Iraq. During the third troop rotation of Operation IRAQI FREEDOM (OIF) from October 2004 to September 2005, the 1st Battalion, 24th Infantry (1-24 IN), a unit equipped with the Stryker wheeled armored vehicle, was responsible for the congested western half of Mosul as part of the 1st Brigade, 25th Infantry Division. Almost immediately after its arrival in November 2004, the 1-24 IN was faced with a chaotic situation when insurgents attacked all the police stations in the battalion's sector and, in one swoop, virtually destroyed Iraqi civil authority and law enforcement capabilities. The battalion responded to this crisis with a decidedly offensive and proactive posture in the execution of counterinsurgency operations which proved to be highly successful. Over the next eleven months, the 1-24 IN would be instrumental in the restoration of western Mosul and in turning Mosul back into the model city it had been touted as prior to the insurrection of November 2004.[2] The effectiveness of the battalion was noted in various media sources at the time and after the battalion's redeployment to Fort Lewis, Washington.[3] Accordingly, this brief study examines the battalion's operations during its tour in Mosul.

Mosul was established since ancient times on the west bank of the Tigris River, opposite the ruins of Nineveh, the capital of the ancient Assyrian Empire. It was an important trading center on the main caravan trade route between India and Persia and the Mediterranean before the completion of the Suez Canal in the nineteenth century. In the twentieth century it became a gateway to the oil fields discovered to the northeast of the city.

Mosul grew up on both sides of the Tigris and by 2003, with an estimated 1.7 million people, was the third-largest city in Iraq (after Baghdad and Basra) and the largest city in the northern third of the country.[4]

The city was a melting pot, with large Kurdish, Christian (Assyrians and Chaldeans) and Turkmen minorities. By 2004, Sunni Arabs had majority status in the city, the result of a combination of factors including a Baathist regime Arabization resettlement policy commencing in the 1970s. The portion of Mosul west of the Tigris River was predominately Sunni Arab, while the portion east of the river, the newest part of the city which, ironically, also contained the ruins of ancient Nineveh, contained most of the Kurdish population.[5]

The half of the city west of the Tigris, for which the 1-24 IN was responsible, consisted of the oldest sections of Mosul, including the provincial and municipal government building district, and several neighborhoods considered to be hotbeds of Sunni insurgent activity. A number of key roads intersected at the Yarmuk Traffic Circle which was northwest of the old city. The neighborhoods around this important intersection would be the center of most insurgent and counterinsurgent activities in the time the 1-24 IN was conducting operations in Mosul. Five bridges crossed the Tigris in Mosul. Instead of referring to them by their specific names, US forces used the shorthand of calling the bridges by number from south to north. The bridges were key lateral terrain features as they connected western Mosul to the eastern districts. The second of these bridges was located adjacent to the government district and the third extended the major downtown thoroughfare called Nineveh Street across the Tigris. Iraqi National Route 1, a divided highway, also known to the US forces as Main Supply Route (MSR) TAMPA, ran north-south through western Mosul. At the Yarmuk Circle, it veered to the northeast, crossing the Tigris over the fifth bridge and proceeded through the northeastern Mosul suburbs towards the Turkish border. Also from the Yarmuk Circle, MSR SANTA FE proceeded to the northwest towards the Syrian border and the city of Tal Afar. Iraqi National Route 2 (or the portion of MSR SANTA FE southeast of Mosul) proceeded from Mosul to Arbil and Kirkuk to the east, crossing the Tigris over the second bridge and in western Mosul, marking the southern edge of the old city area.[6] The older portion of western Mosul, next to the river, was densely populated with narrow streets and closely packed buildings. Newer districts, extending to the north, south and west of the old city, while still urban, also had a mix of industrial and residential areas, with wider streets, better facilitating the maneuver of military vehicles.[7]

Three miles from the old city, on the southwestern edge of Mosul, was the large municipal airport. US forces turned the airport and an adjacent Iraqi military compound called Camp Ghazlani into a large base camp complex. The airbase was christened Logistics Support Area Diamondback. The former Iraqi military complex had several different names, ultimately being called Forward Operating Base (FOB) Marez. Marez, located on a hill overlooking Mosul from the south, had a long history as an Iraqi military installation. During the British mandate, the post was known as Tank Hill Camp. In the Baathist era, a portion of the camp, known as Salammiyah Camp, was the headquarters of the Iraqi Fifth Corps, which had commanded all Iraqi army forces in northern Iraq. These two base camps would become the main cantonment for the US forces operating in western Mosul (and, in some cases, elsewhere in Nineveh Province) and the main logistics hub for the whole multinational force in northwestern Iraq. [8]

Mosul was not directly involved in the major combat operations of March and April 2003. On 11 April, the Iraqi 5th Corps surrendered to a joint Kurdish-American force. A small force of Marines then arrived in the city and set up a base at the airport. The first substantial American presence in the city was the deployment of a brigade of the 101st Airborne Division (Air Assault) on 20 April 2003, followed by the bulk of the division within a few days.[9]

While Mosul went through the various troop rotations of Operation IRAQI FREEDOM from 2003 to 2006, the city also went through several cycles of turmoil and stability. Initially, during the OIF-I deployment under the 101st Airborne Division, the city was fairly calm except for the firefight which resulted in the deaths of Uday and Qusay Hussein in July 2003. This stability continued into the OIF-II deployment, even though the 101st was replaced in early 2004 in Nineveh Province by only a brigade-sized force, the 3d Brigade, 2d Infantry Division, out of Fort Lewis, Washington. The 3d Brigade was the Army's first unit equipped with the Stryker wheeled armored combat vehicle. [10]

At the very end of the OIF-II deployment, Mosul erupted in a frenzy of violence which roughly coincided with the I Marine Expeditionary Force's joint assault on the city of Fallujah in Anbar Province, November 2004. Sunni insurgents had seemingly massed in the Mosul metropolis in response to the pressure at Fallujah. This terrorist escalation soon saw the collapse of the local Iraqi law enforcement agencies, creating a crisis on the city streets. The rise of instability in Mosul coincided with the routine rotational turnover among the American forces between OIF-II and OIF-

III units. A new Stryker brigade had arrived to replace the departing 3d Brigade. The newcomers, also from Fort Lewis, were the 1st Brigade, 25th Infantry Division, which included the 1-24 IN.[11]

The 1-24 IN was a unit whose members had minimal combat experience prior to arrival in Mosul. The unit had been stationed at Fort Lewis since 1991 and had received its current designation in August 1995. In October 1999, then-Army Chief of Staff GEN Eric Shinseki had announced the transformation of two light infantry brigades stationed at Fort Lewis into a medium brigade equipped with a yet-to-be-fielded wheeled vehicle. One of these brigades was the 1-24 IN's parent unit, the 1st Brigade, 25th Infantry Division. The wheeled vehicle was developed and later named the Stryker after two Army Medal of Honor winners. The brigade had been slated to become the second Stryker unit and, starting in the spring of 2002, had converted from a light infantry configuration to the new Stryker brigade organization.[12]

The Stryker was designed to provide a single solution to the mobility and survivability weaknesses of light infantry and the deploy-ability problems of mechanized infantry and armor units. It is an eight- wheeled armored vehicle which comes in various configurations such as infantry carrier, reconnaissance, command, medical and signal. All the variants weighed less than 19 tons, easing air deployment concerns. Most variants were equipped with a turret-mounted .50-caliber machine gun or MK19 automatic grenade launcher. Modern digital communications and information packages were an integral part of the Stryker package.[13] One variant of the Stryker, the mobile gun system (MGS), was not fielded. In Stryker units, MGS Strykers were instead equipped with the TOW anti-armor guided missile system. To combat the extensive insurgent use of the shaped charges fired from rocket propelled grenade (RPG) weapons against American vehicles, Strykers deployed to Iraq were retrofitted with an external wire skirt called slat armor. The development and deployment of the Strykers was considered controversial, but the vehicle proved to be quite operationally effective in the urban environment.[14]

Despite having few combat veterans in the unit, 1-24 IN, or "Deuce Four" (the unit's longtime, unofficial nickname), was relatively well prepared for its yearlong deployment to Mosul. The battalion had trained extensively for the mission. This included participation in a highly successful rotation at the Army's Joint Readiness Training Center (JRTC) at Fort Polk, Louisiana, and the completion of a training regimen that included complicated platoon live-fire exercises and leader development instruction which emphasized civil affairs aspects.[15]

In mid-October 2004, the 1-24 IN conducted a relief in place with the Stryker battalion from the 3d Brigade, 2d Infantry Division, which had been previously responsible for western Mosul, the 1st Battalion, 23d Infantry. The situation in Mosul at the time of the 1-24 IN's arrival was directly affected by two major events. The first of these was the upcoming Iraqi election in January 2005. The voters in this election were to select representatives who would then draft a new national constitution. The insurgents, particularly those of Sunni Arab background, were expected to oppose the conduct of the election vigorously. Accordingly, in areas of Iraq expected to be problematic, security was to be tight. However, Mosul was not originally considered to be one of these areas.

The second event was the conduct of a major offensive operation by a combined and joint force of Marines, soldiers and Iraqi Security Forces personnel to eradicate the insurgent stronghold in Fallujah in early November. Intelligence analysts estimated that a force of between 2,000 and 3,000 insurgents was entrenched in the city. The Fallujah operation was conducted to clear that major Sunni city so that the electoral process could take place there as well as everywhere else in Iraq. The operation ended up lasting several weeks.

While the Fallujah attack itself had few direct repercussions in the Mosul area, preparations for it did, which saw two key measures that would affect the course of events in the northern city. The first of these was the interim Iraqi government's declaration of a national state of emergency for sixty days, commencing on 7 November. The declaration allowed for the rapid imposition of martial law, including curfews and other high-security measures, in particular areas. Martial law was immediately declared in Fallujah and the neighboring city of Ramadi. Mosul remained, for the time being, unaffected by this measure. The second measure was the cordoning off of Fallujah in the weeks before the assault. Such obvious preparations had a two-fold effect on the insurgency: the insurgent leadership sought other places from which to operate in lieu of its Fallujah stronghold; and they sought to open new points of conflict to divert coalition forces from the Fallujah battle. Mosul, with its large urban area and sizeable Sunni population, more than fit the bill as a replacement for or diversion from Fallujah.[16]

The potential vulnerability of Mosul, with its largely untested Sunni police and Iraqi Security Forces (ISF) elements, remained unrecognized by the Coalition leadership. When the 1st Brigade, 25th Infantry Division, rotated into the city, it was immediately ordered to detach one of its Stryker battalions to reinforce the Fallujah attack. The 1st Battalion, 5th Infantry, was dispatched to the south in order to add the unique abilities of the Stryker to the attacking force. The rest of the brigade, including the 1-24 IN, assumed watch over their respective sectors in Mosul and throughout the bulk of Nineveh Province.[17]

The 1st Battalion, 24th Infantry, organized under the Stryker battalion structure, consisted of a headquarters and headquarters company (referred to as Hatchet) and three infantry (or line) companies, A or Apache, B or Bulldog, and C or Cobra. Each line company contained fourteen infantry Stryker vehicles and was organized into three infantry platoons. Each platoon had four infantry Strykers. There was also a mobile gun system platoon equipped with three Strykers armed with TOW anti-armor missile systems in each company, a mortar section with two Stryker-mounted 120-mm mortars and a company headquarters consisting of two infantry command Strykers, an ambulance Stryker and a fire support Stryker. At the battalion level, the headquarters company contained a reconnaissance platoon, a mortar platoon with four 120-mm mortars, a medical platoon and a seven-man sniper squad. The battalion headquarters itself had Strykers for the use of the battalion commander and operations officer (S-3) and several other vehicles with specialized communications equipment. The headquarters also included a staff of seven soldiers dedicated to intelligence (S-2) activities.[18]

In the autumn of 2004, the Iraqi Security Forces and police were in a state of flux. The Iraqi Army consisted of only three divisions, while the separate Iraqi National Guard (ING) was slated to be seven divisions. Both forces were at various stages of organizational development. In the Sunni Arab sections of Mosul, a deliberate attempt had been made to employ Iraqi soldiers and policemen with Sunni backgrounds. The pre-existing police forces had been retained and used in joint foot patrols almost from the start. In July 2004, immediately after national sovereignty was returned to the Iraqis, the governor of Nineveh Province planned and executed a large, joint police-Iraqi National Guard operation in a troubled neighborhood of Mosul.[19]

The weakness of the local police forces had been obvious since early 2004 when the insurgents began to specifically target them. In April, insurgents tried to overrun the city government buildings and several police stations. Many policemen melted away and US forces had to restore the situation. On 24 June, four simultaneous car bombs killed 29 policemen and wounded another 70, while two police stations were abandoned. The US and Iraqi troops had to counterattack and regain control of the two stations.[20]

48

Forming at the former Al Kindi missile facility, northeast of Mosul, the ING's 2d Division consisted both of units composed completely of Kurdish and Sunni Arab members and units of a more mixed composition. For the most part, the Kurdish units, the majority consisting of experienced soldiers, did not patrol the Sunni Arab sections of Mosul, these being left to newly raised Sunni Arab units. A brigade-sized ISF element (three battalions) patrolled or operated out of western Mosul, along with about 2,500 members of the police forces who operated five of Mosul's ten Stations, including the main city police headquarters.

The enemy, or Anti-Iraqi Forces (AIF), in the Mosul area in 2004 and 2005 consisted of six distinct insurgent groups. Five of these were groups of Islamic extremists, each with slightly different goals and beliefs. One of these groups claimed affiliation with Al Qaeda. All these elements were fanatical in their commitment to the cause and usually worked together for the common goal. Apart from these fundamentalists, there was also a group of former regime elements (FREs), somewhat less fanatical Sunni Baathists, operating to destabilize the new government. Accordingly, the FRE primarily targeted the representatives of the new Iraqi government. The FRE and extremists only worked in concert when they had to, otherwise being at odds with each other. Estimates for the size of insurgent forces in Mosul were between 400 and 500 active fighters, supported by, perhaps, 2,000 to 2,500 part-time or intermittent members. While these forces were fragmented, and the FRE was at odds with the rest, the AIF did seem able to coordinate operations occasionally, particularly during the pre-election offensive in November 2004.[21]

In the months before the arrival of the 1-24 IN in Mosul, the enemy use of improvised explosive devices (IEDs) and vehicle-borne IEDs (VBIEDs) seemed to be increasing in the city. There was also an increased number of direct-fire contacts with the AIF. Many of them were the result of proactive patrols seeking out the cells emplacing IEDs. As mentioned above, the AIF had started to direct its efforts against the ISF units in Mosul and were mounting larger and more coordinated attacks against the local Iraqi forces. These trends continued as 1st Brigade, 25th Infantry Division, replaced 3d Brigade, 2d Infantry Division, on the streets of Mosul. When the new American unit arrived in western Mosul, it was bombarded with mortar shells. After patrols took out the mortar cells, the insurgents began attacking Iraqi civilians and attempting to take de facto control of portions of the city starting with a large-scale attack on 10 November.[22]

As the 1-24 IN settled into its sector of Mosul in October 2004, the battalion had able, experienced leadership. The battalion commander,

LTC Michael Erik Kurilla, a 1988 US Military Academy graduate, was an experienced infantry officer who had served in the 1989 invasion of Panama, DESERT STORM, Haiti, Bosnia, and Kosovo. Kurilla had commanded the battalion for five months. His key subordinates were also experienced officers and included executive officer MAJ Michael Lawrence, who ran the battalion's base at FOB Marez, operations officer (S-3) MAJ Mark Bieger, who spent most days in the city coordinating and fine-tuning operations, and CSM Robert Prosser. Battalion intelligence (S-2) activities were directed by CPT John Jodway. The company commanders had been in their positions prior to deployment and included CPTs William Jacobsen (Apache), Robert Shaw (Bulldog), Chris Hossfeld (Cobra), and Matthew McGrew (Hatchet).

The battalion area of operations (AO), about 800 square kilometers, included all of Mosul west of the Tigris River, a large expanse of uninhabited desert to the west of the city, and a dozen small towns also west of the city. This expanse included two major routes (codenamed BARRACUDA and SANTA FE) leading to Tal Afar. The battalion's mission was to find, fix, and destroy all hostile forces. Each of the three companies was given an AO within the battalion sector. These AOs were within western Mosul. Apache Company's sector included the densely populated, old city area and a cluster of government buildings. Bulldog Company had a sector of northern Mosul, and Cobra had responsibility for the southwestern portion of the city. While Bulldog and Cobra's AOs included portions of desert adjacent to the city, the bulk of the area west of the city was retained under battalion control. Units from the battalion operated in this area, as needed, as an economy of force measure. Since the ISF elements in Mosul had yet to be assigned specific American adviser teams, the HHC commander, CPT Matthew McGrew, had the special mission of being the battalion's lead adviser and coordinator with the ISF forces, using several soldiers from the battalion mortar platoon to fill out his ad hoc team. The bulk of the mortar platoon either provided fire support, or acted as convoy escorts depending on current requirements. The battalion reconnaissance platoon provided security for the battalion commander's tactical command post (TAC), which moved throughout the battalion AO on a daily basis. Additional TACs were organized at both the battalion and company levels and, with the firepower of their Strykers, became virtually separate maneuver elements. Companies typically divided their own sectors into platoon AOs and each platoon was tasked to become familiar with the people, police, and ISF within their sectors. However, most company and some battalion-level operations crossed both platoon and company sector boundaries.[23]

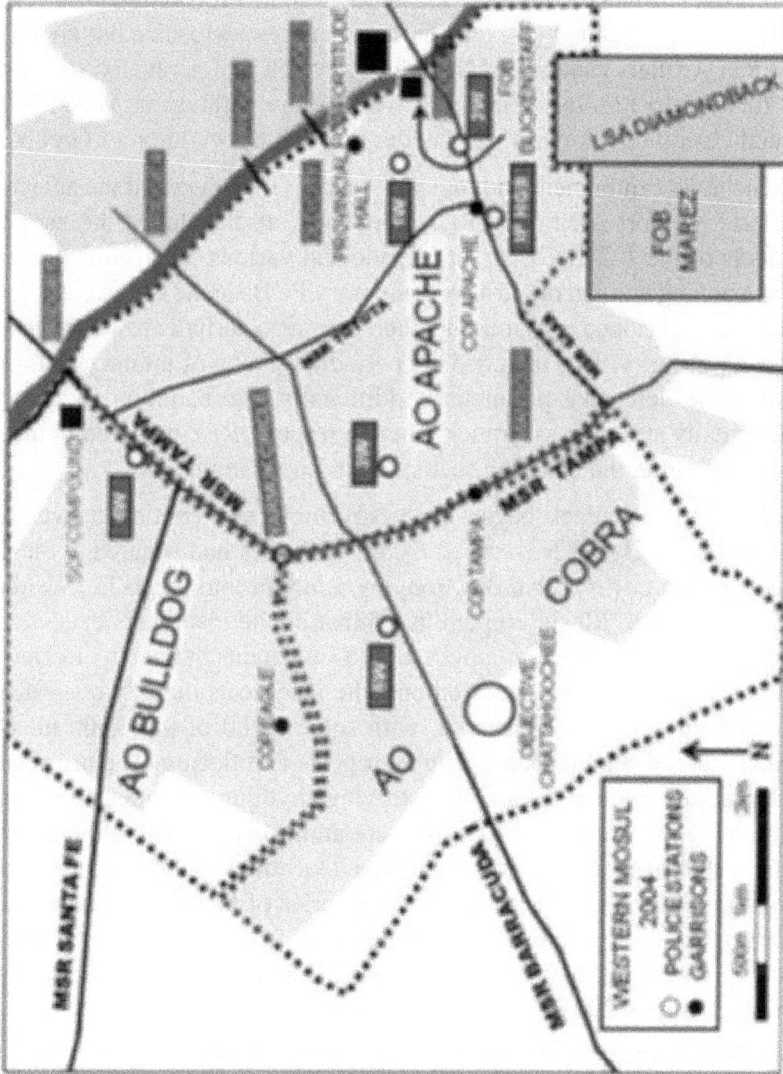

Map 4. The Western Mosul Area of Operations.

The parent brigade of the 1-24 IN, the 1st Brigade, 25th Infantry Division, was headquartered at a former Saddam Hussein palace complex called Camp Freedom in northern Mosul, east of the Tigris. Task Force Olympia, the controlling headquarters for the brigade and other forces in Nineveh Province, was also located at Camp Freedom. The brigade placed another battalion (3-21st Infantry) in eastern Mosul, a battalion (2-8th Field Artillery) south of Mosul at Qayyarah and a cavalry squadron (2-14th Cavalry) at Tal Afar to the west. Also operating in Mosul were Special Operations Forces (SOF) under the 10th Special Forces Group.[24]

The large cantonment and logistics base, FOB Marez and the adjacent Logistics Support Area (LSA) Diamondback, also included the support elements of the 1-24 IN's parent brigade and various other units. Except when manning combat outposts or temporary FOBs in the city, Deuce Four units were garrisoned at Marez and, therefore, also partially responsible for the post's security. This included the periodic rotation of infantry platoons through the defensive perimeter. Additionally, the battalion retained a platoon daily at Marez as a quick reaction force (QRF), prepared to move anywhere within the battalion sector at a minute's notice.[25]

The Fallujah attack began on 8 November and continued over the next two days. By 10 November, Coalition forces had secured about 70 percent of the city. On that day, roughly a month into the 1-24 IN's tour of duty, however, Mosul erupted in combat as the insurgents executed a mass attack against the Iraqi police and ISF elements in the city. In Deuce Four's AO, of the five police stations, the insurgents quickly overran all but the main police headquarters, with some 3,200 of the 4,000 mostly Sunni Arab policemen abandoning their posts and fleeing. The insurgents ransacked the stations, taking or destroying anything of value and usually abandoning the station. ISF patrols were ambushed as well, although the focus of the enemy attacks was on the fixed locations of the police stations. The AIF followed up this success with a series of large-scale attacks and efforts to control whole Mosul neighborhoods. It also executed terror campaigns designed to intimidate the local population in the weeks leading up to the January 2005 elections.[26]

Kurilla and the 1-24 IN responded to the crisis in their AO with characteristic aggressiveness and optimism. By midday on 11 November, the Iraqi provincial governor asked for American assistance and the Deuce Four commenced clearing operations in southwestern Mosul. The massed insurgents fought back and soon Apache Company, supported by other battalion elements, was in a six-hour firefight with a force of more than

60 AIF members which ended in the destruction of the insurgent force.[27] On 14 November, a force composed of Iraqi police commandos, elements of the neighboring Stryker battalion (3-21st Infantry) and a Deuce Four Apache Company QRF platoon repelled an insurgent attack on the 4-West police station in the northern portion of western Mosul. The retaking of 4-West marked the return of control of all Mosul police stations to Coalition forces.[28]

The weeks before the January election were the most intense period of activity in western Mosul. In trying to thwart the electoral process, the enemy countered 1-24 IN aggressiveness with head-to-head firefights and large ambushes throughout December. Almost every patrol would make contact several times every day. Soon contacts had risen from a daily low of 3-4 six months earlier to 25-35 a day.[29] The culmination of these large battles was the action at Combat Outpost (COP) Tampa on 29 December. Aside from that action, the most significant enemy attack took place right on FOB Marez itself when, on 21 December, a suicide attacker detonated a bomb inside the main dining facility, killing 22 soldiers, including the Apache Company commander, CPT William Jacobsen. Subsequently, CPT Jeffrey Van Antwerp became the new Apache commander. This setback clearly illustrated the difficulty in detecting terrorists who could hide even among post support workers and the dangerous capabilities the enemy possessed.

Meanwhile, ISF reinforcements arrived in Mosul. After the destruction of the civil police in western Mosul, the Iraqi government moved Kurdish forces in from the 2d ING Division and several elite battalions from the Iraqi Army's Intervention Force (IIF), as well as a brigade of special police commandos. While the Kurdish battalions remained on the east side, Sunni units from the IIF and ING, as well as a unique mixed Sunni Arab-Kurd ING unit patrolled western Mosul. These forces remained in Mosul to provide additional security for the elections and worked beside the Deuce Four on joint patrols while the police were reconstituted.[30]

Despite the setbacks of November and the attack at FOB Marez, counteroffensive and enhanced security operations continued. With each major firefight, the AIF suffered heavy losses, which would soon force a change of tactics. The counteroffensive phase of the 1-24 IN's Mosul tour ended with the Iraqi elections on 30 January 2005. The restoration of public order and stability since November was so marked that the Sunni Arab neighborhood of Mansour, in southwest Mosul, had the highest voter turnout in Mosul.[31]

Kurilla had several options to respond to the collapse of civil authority in western Mosul. He could continue with the types of patrolling actions his companies had been performing prior to the insurgent offensive. While this choice was the most conservative and safest for the American troops, it had proven unable to prevent the massive insurgent attack in November. However, it allowed the 1-24 IN to retain the initiative and could now prove to be effective if the enemy had suffered heavily, as was thought, in the Coalition counteroffensive.

The 1-24 IN could also set up temporary outposts within the city that were continually shifted. This alternative allowed the unit the ability to mass or shift forces against areas of increased insurgent activity while maintaining the initiative. However, the unit would be spread thinly throughout the city and the temporary bases would not be as survivable as the main FOB and would require a certain amount of effort to build, tear down, move, and rebuild.

Finally, Kurilla could establish permanent outposts within the city within each company sector, generally positioned in the most important or dangerous areas. While such an option would decrease Kurilla's flexibility and spread his unit out somewhat, it had a couple of advantages. The first of these was that the forward placement of troops would place the Americans out among the city's populace, one of the tenets of counterinsurgency doctrine. Another advantage was that the garrisons would create survivable positions. Forward deployed troops would be able to fight from good defensive positions rather than be caught out in the open in an ambush. A clear disadvantage was that the creation of static defensive positions gave the enemy the initiative and created multiple targets for the insurgents to attack. Convoys dispatched to resupply the outposts, given the need to use obvious routes, could also become targets of ambushes. Kurilla could mitigate the potential loss of initiative by using the new bases as remote sites from which to conduct aggressive patrolling.

Kurilla decided that the 1-24 IN needed to retain a permanent presence at key points within Mosul. Accordingly, each company established platoon-size combat outposts within the company AOs on main supply routes. Apache established a full-time presence at the Provincial Hall, the government complex in the old city section of Mosul. Bulldog established COP Eagle along MSR SANTA FE northwest of Yarmuk Circle. To the west of Provincial Hall, Cobra established COP Tampa on MSR TAMPA at a key crossroads on the outskirts of the old city area in the heart of the Mosul neighborhood considered to be the insurgents' stronghold. The outpost was placed in a four-story concrete building which had previously been used by the AIF.[32]

The Americans did not have to wait long for the insurgent response to the new strategy. On 29 December 2004, after almost two months of devastating losses, the enemy leadership decided to try one more large operation in western Mosul, an operation designed to attack and destroy one of the new American strong points and use it as bait to ambush the expected relief column. The result was the action at COP Tampa, which is recounted in great detail elsewhere. Cobra Company and Kurilla's tactical command post successfully repulsed the fierce attack with only one American soldier killed in action (KIA). Abu Musab al-Zarqawi's AIF planners had apparently hoped to destroy a complete Stryker platoon and its outpost and the 1-24 IN command group in a single stroke. The well-planned and coordinated operation would be the last such action employed by the AIF against the 1-24. This action, coupled with the success of the elections a month later, were the turning points in the 1-24's fight in Mosul.[33]

After the elections, AIF actions reverted to a smaller-scale insurgency, with sniper attacks and roadside and car bombs, rather than large ambushes or firefights. The 1-24 IN command team had a few minor changes in the stability phase. In April 2005, the Bulldog Company commander, CPT Robert Shaw, was wounded in a car bomb attack that also fatally wounded the company's 1SG Michael Bordelon. CPT Paul Carron replaced Shaw. Bordelon's replacement, 1SG Brian Hamm, was also wounded in May. Cobra Company's commander, Christopher Hossfeld, went on rest and recuperation leave in April and rotated out to the brigade staff to be replaced by CPT Scott Cheney.

In the stability phase of operations, Deuce Four battle rhythm consisted of a complex series of interlocking daily operations designed to restore security to the residents of Mosul, assist in the development of the ISF and police, and to develop intelligence. The battalion averaged about 30 combat patrols and four raids daily. Platoons (infantry and MGS) would typically execute one patrol in the early morning and a second in the early evening; Raids were generally conducted at night, based on fresh intelligence information, and averaged between two to four operations a week. Platoons originally conducted about eight hours of combat patrolling per day until March 2005. After March, with the ISF assuming some missions and the decline in enemy activity, patrols averaged four to six hours a day. Companies manned combat outposts in their AOs until the January elections were completed. After that, the posts were gradually turned over to ISF units. Each platoon was given a rest day every nine days. The battalion commander and company commanders participated in patrols either with a specific platoon or as an independent TAC element, spending a similar amount of time in the city as did the patrolling platoons. Commanders at all levels were expected to meet local leaders, officials and business leaders on a daily basis.[34]

An illustration of a typical 1-24 IN operation during the stability phase is the 27 April 2005, Operation CHATTAHOOCHEE, conducted by Cobra Company and the 1st Battalion, 3d Brigade, Iraqi Intervention Force (1-3 IIF) on the western edge of Mosul. The 1-3 IIF was considered to be an elite ISF unit. Map 5 shows CPT Scott Cheney's contingency operation (CONOP) briefing slide used to brief his subordinates in preparation for the operation. The slide shows the standard method of presenting an operation to subordinates in the 1-24 IN. The operation was a cordon-and-search operation of a local sheep market where intelligence sources indicated weapons were being transferred to AIF elements. Cobra Company platoons cordoned off the market from all sides, while a company of 1-3 IIF moved south from its base at COP Eagle, accompanied by the C Company TAC. The IIF then executed the search. Although neither a large weapons cache nor many terrorist suspects were found, the operation was successfully executed.[35]

Several factors played key roles in the waning of the insurgency in Mosul. These included the timely development of intelligence, the cooperation between special operations forces and the 1-24 IN's conventional units, and the development of the Iraqi police and the ISF.

For the intelligence mission, the relatively small battalion S-2 section was augmented with brigade and other external assets. When the battalion proved successful at developing intelligence, it received more assets. Deuce Four leaders soon discovered that terrorist detainees spoke freely upon capture and the detention of a particularly well-connected AIF member could result in a goldmine of intelligence and a series of subsequent captures. In order to get the information out of the captured individuals so that it can be used in a timely manner, the battalion built and then expanded a detention facility on FOB Marez.[36]

In support of the conventional units, special operations forces (SOF) from the 10th Special Forces Group, Fort Carson, Colorado, had been operating in Mosul since the beginning of OIF-I in 2003. The SOF elements concentrated on destroying AIF leadership at the highest possible levels. There was complete coordination between the SOF operators and the soldiers of 1-24 IN in the development of intelligence. After the elections, the targeted AIF leadership in Mosul was destroyed. Significant captures included Zarqawi's chief subordinate, Abu Talha, on 14 June, Talha's

Map 5. Plan for Action at Objective CHATTAHOOCHIE, 27 April 2005.

57

replacement, Abu Bara, on 27 July, and eastern Mosul terrorist leader Mullah Mahdi on 3 June.[37]

From the start, LTC Erik Kurilla and the Deuce Four had an additional mission they were not organized to execute. While fighting the AIF, the unit had to train and provide support elements of ISF and Iraqi police in the battalion AO. Headquarters company commander, CPT Matthew McGrew, was given this mission as his primary assignment.

Some ISF units, like the elite battalions of the Iraqi Intervention Force (IIF), serving in Mosul for election security, arrived with American advisers already supporting them but most of the units of the Iraqi National Guard in Mosul would not have advisers or support teams until the summer of 2005.[38] McGrew filled this gap, along with a small number of soldiers detached from their parent companies, and part of the battalion's mortar platoon. Initially, during the counterattack phase, McGrew and his team tried to keep the units together and get them into the fight.[39]

Two Iraqi battalions operating in western Mosul were at first partnered with the 1-24. These were the 22d Battalion, 6th Brigade, IIF, and the 106th Battalion, ING.[40] While he coordinated the integration of the operations of the IIF forces in the 1-24 IN sector through the units' American advisers, McGrew became involved with the operations of the 106th Battalion, garrisoned at Marez, at the Mosul Airport (LSA Diamondback), and in a cantonment just north of Marez called Ghazlani (the former name of Marez when it was a Baathist facility).[41]

After the January elections, emphasis accelerated on training the Iraqi forces to relieve US forces. The initial goal was for Iraqi units to take over some of the FOBs and COPs in the Mosul area. The ultimate objective was for the Iraqis to provide the bulk of the security for the elections in October and December 2005.[42] The first of these handoffs was Apache Company's transfer of security duties at Provincial Hall to the Iraqi police in January 2005. Apache commander Jeffrey Van Antwerp established a new COP called Apache near the junction of two key downtown routes (north-south MSR TOYOTA and east-west MSR SAAB). COP Apache was conveniently near the Mosul police headquarters. At the end of February, COP Apache was handed off to the 106th IA Battalion. Cobra Company handed off COP Tampa to an IIF unit at about the same time and Bulldog gave control of COP Eagle to the 22d IIF Battalion.[43] In March, a sister unit to the 22d Battalion, 6th IIF Brigade, was given a small sector of downtown Mosul.[44]

McGrew had barely begun implementing his training program for the 106th Battalion when things became complicated. The decision had been made to withdraw the 6th IIF Brigade from Mosul by June.[45] The elite brigade was needed in Anbar Province. The IIF units would be replaced by the 4th Brigade, 2d Division, Iraqi Army (IA).[46] The new units had been located in Dahuk and eastern Mosul and, unlike the IIF units they were replacing, did not have assigned American advisers or a Military Transition Team (MiTT). In addition to the 2d Battalion, 2d Brigade, 2d Division (2/2/2 IA) (the former 106th Battalion), the 1-24 IN would support the 4th Brigade headquarters and one of the brigade's organic battalions, the 3d Battalion, 4th Brigade, 2d Division (3/4/2 IA).[47]

To meet this new requirement, McGrew set up an extensive training program. The battalion headquarters was paired with the 4th Brigade headquarters, while Cobra assumed responsibility for 2/2/2 IA and Bulldog for 3/4/2 IA. In June, the 4th Brigade headquarters deployed to FOB Endurance, located across the Tigris over Bridge 1, while 3/4/2 IA took over COPs Apache and Tampa and traffic control points west of Mosul. In July, dedicated MiTT teams arrived for the Iraqi units and McGrew and the 1-24 IN handed off their advisory duties to the newcomers. Upon the transition, the 2/2/2 IA battalion was given a readiness rating of three out of four (four being the lowest). McGrew's team felt the battalion needed another three months of preparation before assuming a sector of responsibility. At the time, the Iraqi battalion was tied into the security of fixed points rather than being capable of offensive operations. However, by the end of 2005, after the redeployment of the 1-24 IN, the battalion was conducting counterinsurgency operations with the rest of its brigade.[48]

Concurrent with the training of the ISF was the rejuvenation of the police forces in western Mosul. After the events of November 2004, the Iraqi Ministry of the Interior retained a special police commando battalion at a former Stryker post from OIF-II in downtown Mosul, FOB Blickenstaff.[49] Restoration of the police force began almost immediately with the appointment of a new police chief, Kahlaf Mohammed Al-Joubouri. Al-Joubouri, a retired Army general, immediately replaced all the police station commanders involved in the November debacle with men he considered trustworthy and competent. He also instituted a program where Mosul officers were trained at the Jordanian Police Academy.[50]

Much of the insurgency in the spring of 2005 was directed against the Iraqi police forces. Despite daily casualties, the Al-Joubouri-led police force stayed on the job and fought back both on the streets and with an informational campaign of two television programs similar to America's Most Wanted. These shows were highly successful as captured insurgents were shown confessing to their crimes and revealed as common criminals and enemies of the state rather than religious warriors. The television shows resulted in a sharp increase in tips reporting insurgent activities.[51]

A particular target was the large 4-West police compound located just north of MSR Tampa west of Bridge 5. The station was key to the counterinsurgency effort because its officers were responsible for security at the main Mosul hospital, a place where insurgents often went after firefights to have their wounds treated. The main attack took place on 18 April when a force of up to 50 insurgents attempted to rout the police at the station. The police held their ground, but the post faced continual mortar shelling, sniper shootings and smaller attacks. After the big attack, 1-24 IN reinforced the garrison and Kurilla visited the station and its aggressive commander, COL Eid Al-Jabouri, daily. Intelligence sources indicated that the insurgent leadership wanted to set a bomb off inside the station. COL Eid was a special target and AIF activities increased whenever Kurilla visited the station. After one of these visits, on 4 August 2005, a sniper killed a soldier from Cobra Company, PFC Nils Thompson, who would be the last Deuce Four soldier to be killed in action in Mosul.[52]

The 1-24 IN's role in the revival of the police was focused on providing support and security as the police established new stations moving westward from the old city into the more dangerous neighborhoods of western Mosul. In April, 2005, one of these, 5-West, was established in the Yarmuk neighborhood southwest of the Yarmuk Traffic Circle. The establishment of this station marked the first permanent police presence in the neighborhood. The new station would soon pay off as its officers destroyed the infrastructure of a local insurgent cell, capturing several key leaders, killing several others, and discovering a large cache of weapons. Three other stations would soon follow in similar neighborhoods.[53]

Despite dire predictions of instability in northern Iraq, the situation in Mosul became more stable in the months after the elections.[54] The success of 1-24 IN in Mosul can be measured statistically. Attacks of all types on Coalition forces in western Mosul declined over 80 percent between November 2004 and August 2005. Mortar attacks reduced from 500 rounds a month to 25; IED incidents decreased by 70 percent; and intelligence reports from Iraqi civilians went from zero to more than 400 per month.[55]

The 1st Battalion, 24th Infantry, earned 181 Purple Heart Medals in Mosul. This is an indicator of the battalion's operational tempo during its 12 month tour. Of the 181, eleven were awarded to soldiers who were either killed in action or died of their wounds. Of the remaining 170, the last soldier wounded in action in the battalion was LTC Erik Kurilla himself. Kurilla used his tactical command post's Strykers as a maneuver force when necessary, leading from the front and taking immediate action against insurgents that came across his path. This approach was seen clearly in the action at COP Tampa on 29 December. On 19 August, Kurilla got involved in close combat with an AIF operative and received wounds that, while not critical, required his medical evacuation out of Iraq. In the same action, CSM Robert Prosser was awarded the Silver Star for subduing the terrorist who had just shot his battalion commander in hand-to-hand combat witnessed by journalist Michael Yon.[56]

On 15 October 2005, the Iraqi public voted to ratify its new constitution. In Mosul, the ISF and police provided almost all of the election security. The 1-24 IN had redeployed on 23 September, handing over western Mosul to another Stryker unit, the 1st Battalion, 17th Infantry, of the 172d Infantry Brigade. The troop rotation had no noticeable effect on election security, most of which being supplied by ISF and Iraqi Police elements.

Nowhere was the success of operations in Mosul more apparent than in the contents of a letter from Abu Zayd, one of the terrorist cell leaders in western Mosul, to terrorist mastermind Musab Zarqawi in July 2005. The letter was captured during a raid on a safe house. Zayd cited the decline in insurgent attacks in Mosul and the replacement of well planned and executed suicide attacks with more but less effective suicide attacks employing poorly trained operatives. The letter showed the distinct lack of leadership and organization now existing in the AIF. The low morale, particularly among the foreign fighter elements in the AIF in Mosul, was also glaring. Part of the insurgent disorganization could be traced directly to the heavy losses in the leadership tier in the months before the elections and the heavy losses in leaders after the elections.[57]

Aggressive, offensive counterinsurgency operations in Mosul were very effective. The commander of the 1st Brigade, 25th Infantry Division, COL Robert Brown, had this to say about the battalion's aggressive pursuit of its mission during its tour in Mosul: "Deuce Four, the thing that made them so unique, they soundly defeated the enemy with direct action and they won the hearts and minds of the people."[58]

Notes

1. Matt Misterek, "Deuce Four's Many Hats," *The* [Tacoma] *News-Tribune*, 18 June 2005, online at http://www.thenewstribune.com/news/military/ stryker/ story/4956128p-4532134c.html, accessed on 24 May 2006.

2. Patrick Cockburn, "Once, They Called it a Model of the Occupation: Has the US Lost Control of Mosul?" *Counterpunch*, 18/19 December 2004, on- line at http://www.counterpunch.org/patrick12182004.html; accessed on12 June2006; Kirsten Lundberg, "The Accidental Statesman: GEN Petraeus and the City of Mosul, Iraq: Epilogue," Kennedy School of Government Case Program C15-06-1834.1, John F. Kennedy School of Government, Harvard, University, Cam- bridge, MA, 2006, 1.

3. The effectiveness of the 1-24 IN has been touted in numerous media reports. Two of the most representative are: Sarah Baxter, "Bruce Willis Comes Out Fighting for Iraq's Forgotten GI Heroes," *The* (London) *Sunday Times*, 27 November 2005, online at http://www.timesonline.co.uk/ article/0,,2089-1892675,00.html; accessed on 12 June 2006; Michelle Tan, "Heavy Mettle Tour: Deuce Four's Extraordinary Commitment to One Another and Their Mission Earned Them Numerous Awards—and Iraqi's Trust." *Army Times*, 27 March 2006: 14-16. The unit was also made famous by the popular internet blog of embedded journalist Michael Yon, http://www.michaelyon-online. com.

4. This is a 2003 population estimate. See "Iraq" in the online version of the *Information Please Almanac*, http://www.infoplease.com/ipa/A0107644.html, accessed on 12 June 2006.

5. Mike Tucker, *Among Warriors in Iraq: True Grit, Special Ops, and Raiding in Mosul and Fallujah* (Guilford, CT: Lyons Press, 2005), 3-4.

6. National Route 2 itself turns north and ultimately reaches the Turkish border.

7. United States Army Infantry School, *Infantry in Battle: From Somalia to the Global War on Terror* (Fort Benning, GA: United States Army Infantry School, 2005), 174-5.

8. FOB Marez was previously known as FOB Glory, Camp Performance and Camp Alabama. It was named in February 2004 after a retired command sergeant major of the 1st Battalion, 23d Infantry, who had recently died. See "18th Engineer Company," *The Arrowhead: Family Readiness Group News-letter*, vol. 7, 22 February 2004: 12, online at http://www.strykernews.com/ docs/021904newsletter.pdf, accessed on 19 June 2006.

9. Kirsten Lundberg, "The Accidental Statesman: GEN Petraeus and the City of Mosul, Iraq," Kennedy School of Government Case Program C15-06-1834.0, John F. Kennedy School of Government, Harvard, University, Cambridge, MA, 2006, 4. The 2d Brigade was actually in Mosul, along with the division headquarters, support units and aviation. The 1st Brigade was at Qayyarrah-West, an airfield about 50 miles south of Mosul and the 3d Brigade was at the Tal Afar airfield about 30 miles west of Mosul.

10. The size disparity was really not that noticeable in Mosul itself. The 101st used a brigade in Mosul with a battalion on each side of the Tigris, as did the follow-on units. The disparity was much more apparent in other parts of Nineveh Province where battalions replaced the other two 101st brigades.

11. LTC Erik Kurilla, e-mail to author, 30 May 2006; LTC Michael Gibler, interview by the Operational Leadership Experiences Project team with the Combat Studies Institute, 8 June 2006, Fort Leavenworth.

12. The 1-24 IN was reflagged from the former 3-9th Infantry at Fort Lewis in August 1995 as part of an Army-wide reflagging campaign which saw the Army reduce in size from 12 to 10 divisions. This change was in conjunction with the replacement of the 1st Brigade, 7th Infantry Division, with the 1st Brigade, 25th Infantry Division, at Fort Lewis. The 1st Brigade, 7th Infantry Division, had been at Fort Lewis since 1994. During the reduction of the Army from 14 to 12 divisions in 1993, the whole 7th Infantry division was designated to move from Fort Ord, CA, to Fort Lewis but this was later whittled down to a brigade with the rest of the 7th Division inactivating. See the following: Jim Tice, "7th ID Soldiers Start Packing Their Bags," *Army Times*, 3 May 1993: 8; Jon Anderson, "Laying Down the'Bayonet': Shutdown of Fort Ord, Inactivation of 7th ID a Massive Heartbreaker," *Army Times*, 13 September 1993: 28; Bernard Adelsberger, "Fort Lewis: Home for Two Heavy Brigades?" *Army Times*, 22 November 1993: 10; Sean Naylor, "The 10-Division Army: All the Details on What Stays and What Goes," *Army Times*, 12 December 1994: 12-13, 16; Sean Naylor, "What's in a Name? Inactivations Stir Memories of Old Soldiers," *Army Times*, 27 February 1995: 8, 10-11; Jim Tice, "All is Said and Done: New Flags for 172 Units," *Army Times*, 3 July 1995: 32, 38, 40, 42-4, 60; Sean Naylor, "Radical Changes: Gen. Shinseki Unveils his 21st-Century Plans," *Army Times*, 25 October 1999: 8.

13. Lester Grau and Elena Stoyanov, "The Bear Facts: Russians Appraise the Stryker Brigade Concept," *Infantry* 93 (November-December 2004): 38-40.

14. Michael Erik Kurilla, "Strykers Get the Job Done," letter to the editor, *Washington Post*, 5 April 2005: p. A22, online at http://www. washingtonpost. com/wp-dyn/articles/A26535-2005Apr4.html, accessed on 7 June 2006.

15. Kurilla, e-mail 30 May 2006. 16. Charles Recknagel, "Iraq: Prime Minister Declares State of Emergency," *Radio Free Europe/Radio Liberty* website, online at http://www.rferl.org/ featuresarticle/2004/11/3ad4c051-062a-495d-ab5c-647537ca837e.html, accessed on 28 July 2006. The state of emergency did not apply to the Kurdish sections in the far northwest of Iraq.

17. There were some signs that all was not well in Mosul before November 2004, primarily a wave of terror killings and signs of the presence of large numbers of foreign fighters in the city. See Andrew Lee Butters, "Losing Mosul? The Northern City Once Hailed as a Post-War Model is on a Perilous Backslide," *Time*, 16 October 2004, online at http://www.time.com/time/ world/printout/0,8816,725055,00.html, accessed on 12 June 2006.

18. Sources for Stryker unit organization include: Department of the Army, *Field Manual 3-21.21, The Stryker Brigade Combat Team Infantry Battalion* (Washington, DC: Department of the Army, 2003); Department of the Army, *Field Manual 3-21.11, The SBCT Infantry Rifle Company* (Washington, DC: Department of the Army, 2003).

19. Lundberg, "Accidental Statesman," 19-21; Michael Tucker, *Among Warriors in Iraq: True Grit, Special Ops, and Raiding in Mosul and Fallujah* (Guilford, CT; Lyons Press, 2005), 27; James Reynolds, "Eyewitness: US Revises Mosul Plans" *BBC News*, online at http://news.bbc.co.uk/ 1/hi/world/middle_east/4036181.stm, accessed on 1 June 2006; Ann Scott Tyson, "Iraqi-led Security Missions Begin." *Christian Science Monitor*, 2 July 2004, online at http://www.csmonitor.com/2004/0702/p06s02-woiq.html, accessed on 29 July 2006.

20. Tyson, "Iraqi-led Security Missions Begin."

21. Michael Yon, "The Battle for Mosul: Dispatch II," *Michael Yon On-line Magazine,* 21May 2005, online at http://www.michaelyon-online.com/wp/the-battle-for-mosul-dispatch-ii.htm, accessed on 1 June 2006. These extremist groups were were Abu Musab al-Zarqawi's Al Qaeda affiliated *Jama'at Al-Tawhid wa Al-Jihad, Ansar al-Islam, Al-Jihad,* and the *Mujahidin Shura* Council and the *Ansar Al-Sunnah* Army. The latter organization took credit for the 21 December bombing of the FOB Marez dining facility. See Michael Knights, "Northern Iraq Faces Increased Instability in 2005," *Jane's Intelligence Review*, February 2005:32, online at http://www.washingtoninstitute.org/ opedsPDFs/4216175bf103e. pdf, accessed on 7 July 2006; Gibler interview.

22. Knights, "Northern Iraq Faces Increased Instability in 2005;" Michael Yon, "The Battle for Mosul." *Michael Yon Online Magazine*, 14May 2005, online at http://www.michaelyon-online.com/wp/the-battle-for-mosul.htm, accessed on 1 June 2006.

23. Jeffrey Van Antwerp, e-mail to author, 3 June 2006; Jeffrey Van Antwerp "AO Apache." PowerPoint slide. 3 June 2006; Scott Cheney e-mail to author, 25 June 2006; Scott Cheney, "C 1-24 Boundaries." PowerPoint slide. 25 June 2006; Matthew McGrew, e-mail to author, 24 July 2006.

24. Gibler Interview. When the 1st Battalion, 5th Infantry, returned from Fallujah, it operated primarily in the Palestinian area of southeastern Mosul and at various places outside the city.

25. Van Antwerp, e-mail, 3 June 2006.

26. Knights, 30-33; Yon, "The Battle for Mosul."

27. "Deuce Four Fallen Warriors," *Stryker Brigade News*, 21 February 2005, online at http://www.strykernews.com/archives/2005/02/21/deuce_four_ fallen_ warriors.html, accessed 31 August 2006.

28. Gibler interview.

29. Kurilla, e-mail 30 May 2006; Knights, 32-3. A brief timeline of large actions involving the 1-24 IN in November-December 2004 follows:

14-29 November	Ongoing campaign to regain control of Mosul nets 43 insurgent detainees.
1 December	Large gun battle.
3 December	Three hour firefight on Route Tampa against 2km-long ambush.
11 December	Rocket and mortar attack at checkpoint, followed by unsuccessful ambush results in first silver star awarded to 1-24 IN member, SSG Shannon Key.
21 December	Homicide bomber attacks dining facility at FOB Mosul, killing 22, including two 1-24 Infantry soldiers, one being A Company commander, CPT William Jacobsen.
28 December	Insurgents tried to seize a western Mosul police stations and are repelled, primarily by ISF elements; this was the ninth such unsuccessful attempt since 10 November.
29 December	Action at COP Tampa.

30. The 1-5 IN, the Stryker battalion dispatched to Fallujah, was recalled immediately. Additional US forces sent to Mosul for election security including 2d Battalion, 325th Infantry from 82d Airborne Division and 1st Battalion, 14th Infantry, battalion from 2d Brigade, 25th Infantry Division, which was shifted up from central Iraq. See Van Antwerp, 3 June 2006. TF Tacoma, element of the 81st Infantry Brigade (Mechanized), Oregon National Guard, provided security for LSA Anaconda at Balad Airbase in central Iraq, sent to Mosul to provide pre-election security after the action at COP Tampa. This task force was composed of Company B, 1st Battalion, 185th Armor, a California Army National Guard unit equipped with M1 tanks, B Company, 160th Infantry, A Company, 579th Engineer Battalion (both California Army National Guard units) and several smaller units. For Mosul mission, 2-325 IN attached to TF Tacoma. ARNG portion of TF Tacoma remained in Mosul until it redeployed in March 2005. See "12 February 2005," online at http://iraq-kill-maim.org/ik35/iraq-kill35.htm, accessed on 1 August 2006.

31. Sandra Jonz, "Soldiers Look to Gain, Secure Trust with Iraqis," *Stars and Stripes*, Mideast edition, 28 May 2005. Retrieved from Google cache, 16 May 2006, online at http://www.google.com/search?q=cache:ko3th_Ik5MMJ: www. stripes.com/article.asp%3Fsection%3D104%26article%3D29384+Mosul&hl=en &gl=us&ct=clnk&cd=58; accessed on 16 May 2006.

32. Van Antwerp, e-mail 3 June 2006; Michael Gilbert, "Silver Star Goes to Stryker Soldiers Tested in Iraq," *The* (Tacoma) *News Tribune*, 6 November 2005, online at http://www.thenewstribune.com/news/local/story/5312151p-4814745c. html, accessed on 9 June 2006.

33. According to Army sources, Zarqawi's Al Qaeda in Iraq organization planned and directed operation against COP Tampa. See Gilbert. For COP Tampa, see John J. McGrath, "Action at COP Tampa: Mosul, 29 December 2004," *In Contact! Case Studies from the Long War, Volume I*, William G. Robertson, ed. (Fort Leavenworth: Combat Studies Institute Press, 2006), 33-58; Kurilla, e-mail 30 May 2006; Gilbert.

34. Kurilla, e-mail 30 May 2006; Van Antwerp, e-mail 3 June 2006.

35. Cheney, e-mail 25 June 2006; Scott Cheney, "Objective Chattahoochee," PowerPoint slide, 25 June 2006.

36. Kurilla, 30 May 2006; Michael Yon, "The Battle for Mosul, Part III," *Michael Yon Online Magazine,* 13 June 2005, online at http://www.michaelyon-online.com/wp/the-battle-for-mosul-part-iii.htm, accessed on 1 June 2006.

37. Kurilla, 30 May 2006; "Terrorist Letter Claims Poor Leadership in Mosul," Multi-National Force-Iraq Release A050806, 6 August 2005, available online at http://www.globalsecurity.org/military/library/news/2005/08/mil-050806-mnfi02.htm; accessed on 1 August 2006).

38. The IIF belonged to the Iraqi Army and evolved into its 1st Division. The Iraqi National Guard was merged into the Army in early 2005.

39. Matthew McGrew, e-mail to author, 24 July 2006 ; Matthew McGrew, e-mail to author, 31 July 2006.

40. the 22d Battalion was redesignated as 1st Battalion, 3d Brigade, 1st Division (1/3/1IA). The 106th Battalion was redesignated as 2d Battalion, 2d Brigade, 2d Division (2/2/2IA).

41. Matthew McGrew, "The Way Ahead: Integration of the 2/2/2/IA and the 3/4/2 IA into Deuce Four Operations," PowerPoint Presentation, April 2005; Matthew McGrew, "106th IA Support Structure," PowerPoint Presentation, February 2005; Cheney, e-mail 25 June 2006.

42. McGrew, "The Way Ahead."

43. McGrew, "The Way Ahead;" Van Antwerp, e-mail 3 June 2006.

44. Steve Fainaru, "Handoff to Iraqi Forces Being Tested in Mosul: US Military Is Accelerating Transition," *Washington Post*, 7 April 2005: p. A1, online at http://www.washingtonpost.com/wp-dyn/articles/A32631-2005Apr6.html; accessed on 12 June 2006.

45. The brigade was redesignated as the 3d Brigade, 1st Division, by this time.

46. This unit was formerly designated as the 23d Brigade, ING.

47. This unit was formerly designated the 111th Battalion, ING. McGrew, "The Way Ahead;" McGrew, e-mail 24 Jul 2006; Matthew McGrew, "Transition Readiness Assessment Report, 2d Battalion, 2d Brigade," PowerPoint slide, 25 June 2006.

48. McGrew, "Transition Readiness Assessment Report;" "Iraqi Security Forces, Task Force Freedom Sweep up Terrorists and Weapons," *News Blaze*, 12 December 2005, online at http://newsblaze.com/story/20051212215028nnnn. nb/topstory.html, accessed on 2 August 2006.

49. The unit's designation was the 1st Battalion, 3d Special Police Commando Brigade.

50. Michele A. Uitermarkt, "Iraqi Police Take Stand at Four-West." *The Freedom Post*, 16 May 2005: 6, online at Google cache, http://72.14.203.104/search?q=cache:cD4O608qmlYJ:www.tffpao.org/The-Freedom-Post/050516/freedom%2520post12.pdf+Al-joubouri&hl=en&gl= us&ct=clnk&cd=9, accessed on 7 June 2006.

51. Kurilla, e-mail 30 May 2006.

52. Yon, "The Battle of Mosul, Part III;" Uitermarkt; Michael Yon, "God's Will." *Michael Yon Online Magazine,* 7 August 2005, online at http://www.michaelyon-online.com/gods-will.htm; accessed on 1 June 2006; Bill Roggio, "Al-Qaeda Attacks the Iraqi Police: The Iraqi Security Services are Increasingly the Target of Attacks by Al-Qaeda, as their Effectiveness is Feared." *Threats Watch. org*, online at http://inbrief.threatswatch.org/2006/01/ alqaeda-attacks-the-iraqi-poli/, accessed on 2 August 2006.

53. Richard A. Oppel, Jr. "A New Police Force Emerges from Mosul's Chaos." *New York Times*, 17 August 2005: p. A1, online at Proquest, http://proquest.uni.com/pdqweb?did=88301757&sid=2&Fmt=3&clientld=509 4&R QT=309&VName=PQD, accessed 1 June 2007; McGrew, "The Way Ahead;" Michael Yon, "Battle for Mosul IV," *Michael Yon Online Magazine,*. 4 October 2005, online at http://www.michaelyon-online.com/battle-for-mosul-iv.htm; accessed on 1 June 2006.

54. Knights, 33.

55. Kurilla, e-mail 30 May 2006.

56. Michael Yon, "Gates of Fire." *Michael Yon Online Magazine*. 31 August 2005, online at . http://www.michaelyon-online.com/gates-of-fire.htm; accessed 1 June 2006.

57. "Terrorist Letter Claims Poor Leadership in Mosul."

58. Michelle Tan, "Heavy Mettle Tour: Deuce Four's Extraordinary Commitment to One Another and Their Mission Earned Them Numerous Awards and Iraqi's Trust," *Army Times*, 27 March 2006:15-16.

Clearing the Jihad Super Bowl
Al Qaim District, Anbar Province November 2003

by

Thomas A. Bruscino, Jr.

The Iraqi insurgency began to intensify in the summer and fall of 2003. In March and April, the American-led Coalition had swept through the country, clearing away most resistance with little difficulty. Saddam Hussein's army and police forces disintegrated in the face of the onslaught, leaving the Iraqi countryside lawless. In the vast western province of Anbar — an area roughly the size of Wyoming, sharing a long border with Syria, Jordan and Saudi Arabia — the problem was especially acute. Relatively small numbers of Special Forces units in the Joint Special Operations Task Force-West cleared Anbar in the spring attacks, and then at the end of April began to turn responsibility of the province over to the 3d Armored Cavalry Regiment (3d ACR), then under the command of COL David Teeples but even the highly mobile 3d ACR — equipped with M1 Abrams tanks, M2/3 Bradley fighting vehicles, and Apache, Kiowa, and Blackhawk helicopters — could only cover so much space. Theirs was an economy of force mission; they had to make do with what they had.[1]

Taking advantage of the wide open spaces, extensive borders, the predominantly Sunni Arab population and the lack of governmental or even military authority, insurgency soon began to grow in Anbar. The situation became particularly problematic in the area along the Euphrates River valley, stretching from the Syrian border southwest toward Baghdad. The towns and areas along the river — Rawa, the Qadisiyah Dam, Haditha, Hit, Ramadi, Habbaniyah, and Fallujah — became notorious centers of insurgent violence, and not by coincidence. These Sunni Arab populated areas along the river valley connected those centers, providing insurgents the ability to move from west to east across the country, wreaking havoc as they moved toward the Iraqi capital. In the summer of 2003, units from the 3d ACR saw spikes in insurgent activity throughout the valley.

In the far northwest, the border district of Al Qaim sits along the Euphrates River within Iraq, but on the Syrian border. Al Qaim District consists of five interconnected towns, all on the south side of the river. One of the towns, the district center, is also called Al Qaim. From west to east, they are Husaybah, Karabilah, Sadah, Al Qaim, and Ubaydi (see Map 6, Ubaydi is off the map to the lower right side), with a population of more than 120,000. The main part of Husaybah, the westernmost town, is a rough square, about a kilometer-and-a-half on a side, located about three kilometers south of the river. Just outside the southwest corner of the square is a separate section of government housing, called the "440 Block" by the Americans because it consists of 440 individual apartments. To the north of the 440 Block, the northwest corner of the town sits squarely on the Syrian border and is the site of a border checkpoint. A four-lane paved highway, Route 12, runs through the checkpoint, cuts across the north side of Husaybah — where it is known to the Americans as Market Street — travels along the south sides of Karabilah, Sadah, Al Qaim, and Ubaydi, and follows the Euphrates southwest before joining Route 10 near Ramadi. Sparsely populated reed fields, crisscrossed with dirt roads, make up the territory between the towns and the river. Riverbeds, called *wadi* by the locals, run north-south past the towns and into the Euphrates. In this region, the river makes a series of lazy S-shapes and occasionally splits around sandbars that have grown into sizable islands. A steep cliff ascends from the terrain on the north side of the river, and then flattens out into smaller population centers connected by more dirt roads. On the border, across the Euphrates from Husaybah, is the small Syrian town of Qusaybah.

The post-invasion lawlessness of Iraq was especially acute in the Anbar border towns. When Saddam Hussein's forces abandoned the military, they also abandoned the string of posts along the Syrian border. Foreign-born jihadists, anxious to join the fight against the Coalition, took advantage of the porous borders to enter Iraq. As one such fighter reportedly told a journalist, "We are mujahideen. We come across to buy weapons every few days. We are all one people; we have no borders between us."[2] Within Iraq, former Baath Party officials and military officers sought to help these young zealots wreak chaos by providing weapons and other aid. Prominent among such officials was Abed Hamed Mowhoush, a former general in Saddam Hussein's military, and a man the Americans likened to a 1920s mob boss.[3]

The economic situation on the border compounded the problem. Border towns like those in the Al Qaim region rely on cross-border trade to drive their small economies, but military activities disrupted trade. In addition, a large phosphate plant south of the towns provided 3,000 jobs to local residents, but the war and power shortages had severely limited the plant's operations, leaving thousands of locals jobless. The insurgents and men like Mowhoush recognized the situation and preyed on the economic troubles to stir up even more hostile activity among the impoverished citizens, paying them to take potshots at the Americans. As a result of the

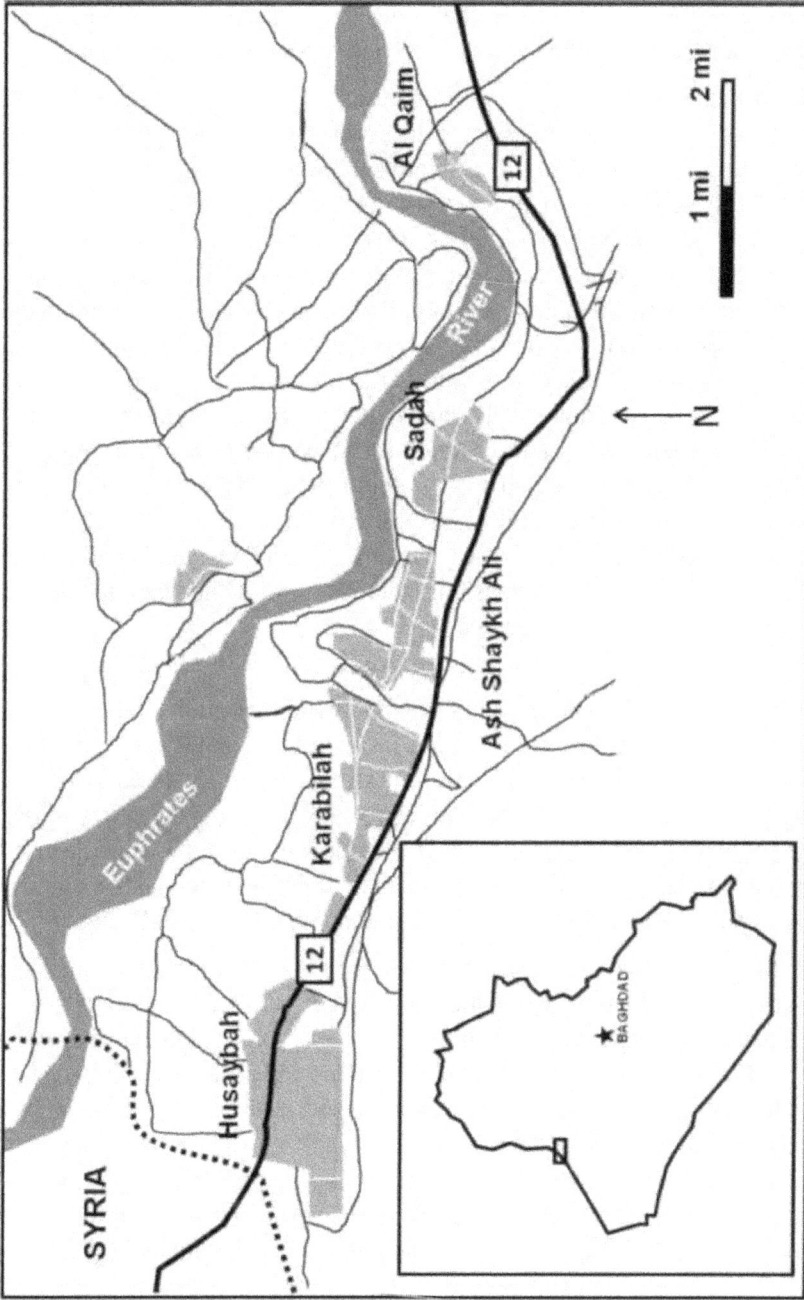

Map 6. Al Qaim District, Anbar Province, Iraq.

71

economic difficulties, open borders, and the activities of former Baathist loyalists, Husaybah and the border towns had become a hotbed of hostile activity and the start of what the Americans called the "rat lines" of insurgent activity stretching from the Syrian border to Baghdad.[4]

Given its complex mission, in the late summer of 2003, the 3d ACR did not have the manpower to pacify the border towns. Originally, the three ground squadrons of the regiment were spread throughout Anbar. The 3d Squadron dealt with the populated area in central Anbar along the river from Hit to Haditha and the highway corridor running from the Euphrates to the Jordanian border. The 2d Squadron worked in the densely populated area in and around Fallujah and Ramadi. The 1st Squadron, commanded by LTC Gregory Reilly, a unit known to the men of the regiment as the Tiger Squadron, was based at a train yard (codenamed Tiger Base) south of Al Qaim, and oversaw the Syrian border area centered on Husaybah. The squadron patrolled a large section of the Syrian border. Reilly's unit was, however, split, with two troops deployed at the key Haditha Dam along the Euphrates in central Anbar, roughly 60 miles east of Al Qaim. The 2d Battalion, 5th Field Artillery Regiment (2-5 FA), attached to the 3d ACR, was assigned various missions, such as training the Iraqi police and eventually the revived Iraqi armed forces.

In August and September, Reilly's squadron began to observe a growing complexity and ferocity in insurgent operations. The enemy had initially used simple tactics, individual firearms, and RPGs to target Americans but by late summer, the insurgents began to include within their ranks more foreigners who had less of a concern for the safety of the local population and infrastructure. These outsiders also developed tactics and weaponry to try to compensate for their fighting disadvantage against the Americans. According to A Troop commander CPT Justin Brown:

> Things had started to pick up tremendously. It wasn't like one or two attacks a day; it was multiple attacks with RPGs and IEDs usually accompanied by some sort of ambush. The IEDs had also become more complicated. It was no longer a single round buried along the side of the road; it was multiple 155 rounds daisy-chained along the side of the road. It was an IED that was used as a primary device to get us to stop. Even dummy IEDs were used to get us to stop and secure an area. They would then place IEDs out further knowing we would get out and try to secure the area to keep people away from the dummy IED, then there would be secondary IEDs set up along the perimeter.[5]

The American patrols continued, and the troops became very proficient at spotting the mines, booby traps, and roadside bombs, which limited casualties. Nevertheless, the intensity of insurgent activity continued to rise. Although the insurgents took shelter in Karabilah and Ubaydi and there were attacks in all of the Al Qaim towns, particularly along Highway 12 in Sadah, Husaybah was the focal point of enemy operations in the area. The city's dense urban environment, its proximity to Syria, and the difficulty of sealing the border, made securing the town all the more complicated.

The arrival in September of the 82d Airborne Division headquarters, led by MG Charles Swannack, with one maneuver brigade in Anbar, brought some relief for the regiment. While the division staff assumed overall responsibility for Anbar, the paratrooper brigade took over from the armored cavalry in Ramadi and Fallujah. Teeples and, in turn, his squadron commanders, could now shift their troops to accommodate the reduced area of responsibility and the rising threat in the Al Qaim area. Teeples' mission was fourfold. First, the regiment had to secure Iraqi Highway 1 running through Anbar to the Jordanian border in order to secure the flow of humanitarian assistance flowing into Iraq from Jordan. Teeples had been using his 3d Squadron for this mission. The 3d Squadron also secured the southernmost Syrian crossing point at Trebil and a major border crossing point with Saudi Arabia at Ar Ar. Part of the squadron was also deployed around the city of Hit. Second, the 3d ACR commander had to secure the Syrian border, particularly the border crossing at Husaybah in the Al Qaim region. As previously mentioned, the 1st Squadron had this mission. The third task facing the 2d Squadron was to provide security for the northern portion of the regimental sector, which included the strategically important Haditha Dam. The large size of this squadron sector forced its commander, LTC Reilly, to split his unit in half between Haditha/Hit and Al Qaim. Before the 82d arrived, Teeples also had the task of securing the heavily populated Fallujah-Ramadi area. He employed his 2d Squadron to do this assignment. The 3d ACR's fourth mission was a general prescription for Teeples to do what he thought best throughout his sector, including patrolling the border with Syria, Jordan, and Saudi Arabia along its extent away from border crossing areas as best he could.[6]

Once the 82d placed a brigade in Ramadi and Fallujah, the 2d Squadron was released for operations elsewhere. Teeples had several options for redeploying his forces. The first of these was to use the 2d Squadron at Hit and Haditha, allowing Reilly to concentrate on Al Qaim. The 3d ACR's 2d Squadron moved to cover the Saudi border and the corridor to the

Jordanian border, and the 3d Squadron focused more intently on the towns along the Euphrates from Anah to Muhammadi, on both sides of Hit. COL Teeples also gave each ground squadron an air cavalry troop of OH-58D Kiowas from the 3d ACR aviation squadron. Still, the growing insurgency focused on the Al Qaim region, and the situation there began to deteriorate in the late summer of 2003.[7]

To add to the difficulty, the soldiers of the 3d ACR had to keep in mind that despite the increased insurgent activity, not everyone was an enemy in the towns. Regimental leadership understood that their mission had become an extremely complex mixture of building relations with local leadership and populations, helping to create and maintain local governments, and constructing infrastructure, all while trying to ferret out enemy forces that had used terror and sympathy to gain a foothold in the border towns. As Reilly later recalled, "Without question, the most difficult challenge of conducting operations in Iraq was finding the right balance between combat operations and non-kinetic stability operations."[8]

In order to gain better control of the situation in that town, Reilly ordered Brown's A Troop, into Husaybah from its position at the border checkpoint. As Brown said, "We're running patrols, but we can't be everywhere. They know we're in this swath, so they just go around us."[9] Many of the enemy fighters ended up in Husaybah, and the men from A Troop, operating out of the border checkpoint, tried to track them down with patrols around the town. Unfortunately, the close quarters of the streets in the interior of Husaybah made it difficult and dangerous for the M1 tanks and Bradley fighting vehicles to move in large sections of the area. And as a heavy armored unit, the troop did not have the strength to dismount and go through the town on foot.

By October, American troops faced multiple daily attacks, and the security situation deteriorated. On 9 October, insurgent gunmen assassinated the local police chief, who had been working with the Americans, while he drove to work in Husaybah. The Iraqi police, frightened for their own safety, abandoned their posts in increasing numbers.[10]

The next day, Reilly wrote in his journal:

> *Something has changed, but it is uncertain what has caused it and why.* The threat is now engaging our forces inside of town during the day and night. Whereas before, the threat would only engage along the outer limits of town, now the threat engages inside of town. This reflects a disregard for collateral damage or danger to innocent people. The enemy is threatening local leaders and has already assassinated the police chief. We are noticing a new TTP,

where attacks are more coordinated with teams operating in concert with each other. The enemy is more willing now to fight longer, firing repeatedly during an engagement. This has resulted in our forces killing several enemies over the last week. We also noticed that the threat is wearing black pants, tennis shoes and shirts, which also suggests the threat is organized and working in teams. This is a new situation and we will need to make adjustments accordingly.[11]

He ordered his B Troop to augment A Troop's efforts in Husaybah by conducting patrols around the clock. Soon the insurgents also started to target those soldiers. On 13 October, a helicopter from the Aviation Squadron was forced to make an emergency landing when enemy fire severed a transmission oil hose. A few days later, Reilly ordered his attached K Battery, which had been previously helping to support the Iraqi police, to garrison the police headquarters in the northeast corner of the city. The squadron instituted a nightly curfew, while A and B Troops patrolled continuously.[12]

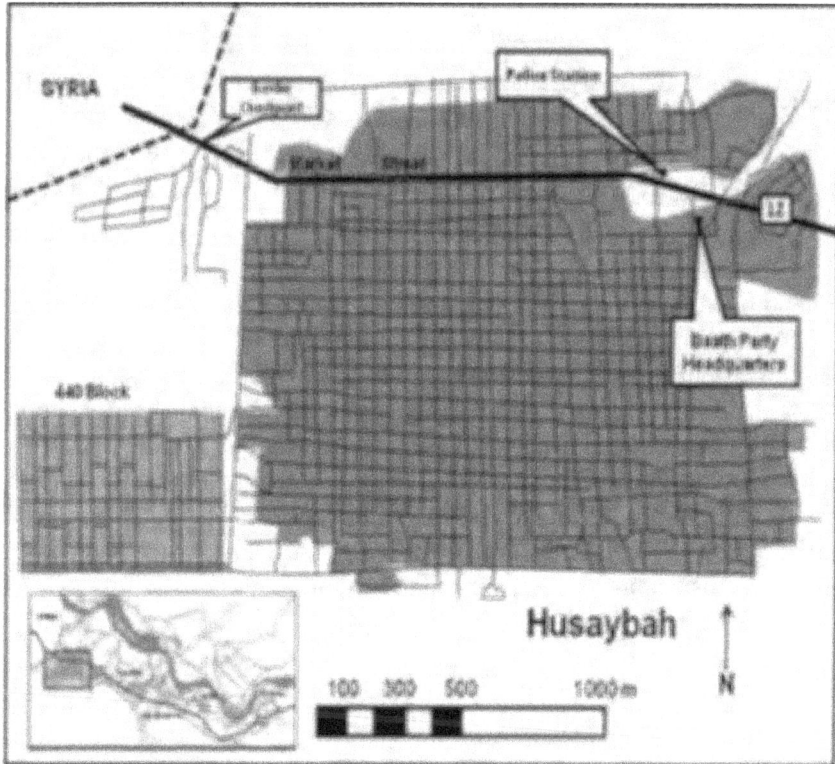

Map 7. Husaybah, Iraq.

Still the violence continued to intensify. The men of Tiger Squadron came under heavy pressure as the insurgents directed mortar and RPG fire on the police station and border checkpoint. Every night from 18 to 21 October, the attacks became more severe and bolder. By 21 October, troops from K Battery had to launch a dismounted attack to pre-empt a coordinated assault on the police station. The following day, Reilly pulled K Battery out of the station, with the intent of repositioning them a few days later at the more easily defended Baath Party headquarters across the street but from the perspective of the locals, it looked like the insurgents had driven the Americans out of the position. When K Battery moved into the Baath party headquarters on 25 October, the Americans came under nearly constant harassing fire. Four days later, B Troop replaced K Battery at the headquarters, and remained there until 9 November.[13] At that time, one platoon leader recalled, "we were attacked on a daily basis in the compound, and at the end we had counted up more than 80 mortars launched at us within one week."[14] Another officer recalled that "it got to the point where [B Troop] was in contact seven or eight times a day. That went on for almost a month solid."[15]

According to Reilly, Tiger Squadron "lost 10 M1A2 Tanks and 10 M3 Bradley's from the period of mid-July to mid-November and after over 200 engagements had not lost a soldier. We hit 41 anti tank mines and received dozens or mortar barrages, so we were very fortunate."[16]

Everyone, from MG Swannack and COL Teeples to LTC Reilly and all of Tiger Squadron's troop and battery commanders, recognized that the situation in Al Qaim had become a problem that required a new solution. On 20 October, a sergeant in Tiger Squadron wrote in his diary, "Husaybah has turned out to be the most dangerous place I have ever been. IEDs, RPGs, land mines, [machine gun] fire every day. After thirteen years in the army, this next one raises the hair on the back of my neck."[17] The men of the 3d ACR, under relentless fire on patrols and at their positions in and around Al Qaim, had begun to call the border towns "The Jihad Superbowl [sic]"[18] The United States Army's efforts in the Al Qaim region had nearly reached a crisis point. Something had to be done.

In the midst of all the spiraling violence, LTC Antonio Aguto, the regimental executive officer, hinted to a reporter that the Army was already working on a response, "You're going to see a greater presence in Al Qaim. That's what's been happening there in the last few weeks."[19] The nature of the American presence would also be new to the region.

LTC Paul Calvert, the 3d ACR's operations officer, remembered:

We had a heck of a lot of resources focused on the border, [and] …
we had tried about every alternative to deny the flow of foreign
fighters into that area of Iraq. We had tried interdiction operations
on the border and surveillance missions on the border. We tried
to break up the cells that were facilitating the movement inside
the Al Qaim region and we did some pinpoint raids and cordon
and searches....[20]

In response to the situation Reilly executed a series of reinforced
squadron-level operations in and around Husaybah in October and
November 2003. The first of these was early October's TIGER STRIKE,
an operation that targeted high-profile figures in the local insurgency. In
TIGER STRIKE, a combination of soldiers from A Troop, B Troop, K
Battery, and attached Special Forces units raided a series of locations in
Al Qaim and detained a total of 120 suspected insurgents.[21] Among the
men detained in the raids were two of Mowhoush's sons. Mowhoush then
turned himself in to Coalition forces in early November in order to gain
clemency for his sons. He later died in captivity after being beaten by Iraqi
forces, transferred to American control and then being placed in a sleeping
bag to coerce information from him. The manner of Mowhoush's death led
to a series of legal and public relations problems for the Army and the 3d
ACR in the months to follow, but his removal as a leader and facilitator of
the insurgency on the ground in Al Qaim proved crucial in the operations
of the fall of 2003.[22]

Next was ALL AMERICAN TIGER, which took place in early
November. That operation also captured several insurgent leaders in the
region, especially in the area between the Al Qaim towns and the river.
Operation ALL AMERICAN TIGER focused on searching and clearing
the farms and villages on the north side of the Euphrates, across the river
from the towns of the Al Qaim District. In the new effort, Tiger Squadron's
C Troop led the way, assisted by a company (B Company, 1st Battalion,
504th Infantry) from the 82d Airborne Division.[23] Unfortunately, C
Troop's commander reported that, "the operation turned up little. The
squadron searched 1,592 houses and found 70 or 80 AK-47s (not unusual)
and several smaller items. The unit as a whole detained 69 men for various
reasons, but most of them were eventually released."[24] Later evidence and
events would show, however, that despite the disappointing numbers, the
operation had, in fact, cleared the area north of the river of insurgent
activity.

In conjunction with ALL AMERICAN TIGER, on 10 November Reilly moved his D Company from border patrolling duties south of Al Qaim into Husaybah. D Company was Tiger Squadron's heavy tank company, consisting of 14 M1A2 Abrams main battle tanks, as opposed to the mix of tanks, Bradleys, and armored mortar carriers that made up the squadron's armored cavalry troops (A, B, and C). CPT Chad Roehrman, the commander of D Company, viewed his command as "the killing force for that squadron. The cav[alry] troops are the ones who are supposed to find and fix the enemy and then the tank company is supposed to finish them."[25] Reilly had the tank company's combat power in mind when he shifted D Company into the town. He told Roehrman, "I need you to go in there and go kinetic to try to bring some security to Husaybah."[26] In addition, Reilly allowed the tank company to use greater force in the city than previous units had been allowed. Specifically, the men of D Company had permission to respond to RPG fire by using the 120-mm high explosive anti-tank (HEAT) rounds from the main guns of their tanks.

While continuing to be based out of the border checkpoint, the tanks of D Company aggressively patrolled the outer perimeter of the town, inviting attacks so that the Americans could return fire on the insurgents. Very quickly the tank crewmen found themselves right in the thick of intense fighting. On the evening of 10-11 November, insurgents twice tried to ambush company patrols. The second, and larger, attack came in the northeast corner of the town as the patrol made a left-hand turn onto Market Street near the police station. D Company's 1SG Daniel Hendrex, saw the action from his seat in a HMMWV:

> ...two RPGs fly over us. Small arms fire started and another tank starts around the corner. I'm firing .50 caliber into the wadi, got the other tank back and get them all on line. I ran out of .50-caliber ammunition because I had used almost 50 percent of my .50-cal[iber ammunition] in the first ambush, but I had an AT-4 [anti-tank rocket] strapped on the HMMWV behind me. As I was pulling it off and getting it set up, that's when two more RPGs from a separate location came in. I just happened to see them as I set the AT-4 up and then shot the AT-4. It was one of those things that was just a miracle shot. I could probably do that a hundred times and it would never happen again. I guess it was just our night. It hit the wall right where they were at and you could clearly see both of them go down. They were about 150 to 200 meters away. As this was happening, we were also directing the second tank that came around the corner into where the first

group of insurgents was and that's when he opened up with main gun. At this point, the tide of the battle turned. We all turned into the ambush. We found out later that there were about 16 men in that ambush and I think we killed three or four.[27]

Just as quickly as D Company found itself in action, it discovered the effectiveness of the use of rounds fired from M1 Abrams tank main gun in the city. A company review after the fight noted that "Collateral damage of a HEAT main gun is not as great as most believe"; however, "No ambush or battle lasted longer than a couple of minutes when HEAT main gun was fired…the effect of a HEAT round fired in [cities] is devastating on the enemy's will to continue the fight."[28] The local population also felt the effect of the increased firepower of the tank main guns. Roehrman remembered:

> the surprised local response in terms of "hey, these guys are actually shooting back – and they're shooting back with tanks, not with just their machine guns!" That got to the point where they actually thought our unit had been replaced. It was one of the funny things we were all laughing about. They thought we were part of the Polish Army because we were actually firing back with tank main gun rounds.[29]

Most of the residents of the town did not seem to resent the use of increased violence because they, too, wanted the insurgents out. A larger number of informants emerged from the local population and the ranks of the local insurgency. For example, on 15 November one such informant led the Americans to a house where they found buried in the courtyard hundreds of Bangalore torpedoes. However, TIGER STRIKE, ALL AMERICAN TIGER, and the more aggressive tactics of D Company did not destroy the insurgency in Al Qaim District.[30]

COL Teeples then decided to conduct a multi-squadron operation, which became known as RIFLES BLITZ, as soon as he could assemble forces. Calvert, recalling the rationale for the decision, cited that such an operation had become the Coalition's "last resort in order to deny these guys the ability to flow foreign fighters into the area and to break up the cells that were operating in the region to facilitate the movement of these guys. This was the culminating event."[31] Swannack and his superiors in Baghdad recognized the importance of the pending offensive and provided Teeples with an air-assault infantry battalion detached from the 101st Airborne Division, which was located in Nineveh Province just to the north of the 3d ACR's area of responsibility.[32]

While 1st Squadron's previous operations had not cleared Husaybah, they had, however, set the stage for RIFLES BLITZ, particularly through the gathering of intelligence. Reilly recalled, "We were gaining so much intelligence we could not act on all of it. When Operation RIFLES BLITZ commenced, we had over 65 target folders to execute…"[33] A planning officer further elaborated:

> Based upon the precursor operations…that had been conducted, we had developed enough of an intel[ligence] picture to where we really felt we had an understanding of the cell that was operating out there, how it was organized and where these folks were but in order to really strike all the targets that had been developed simultaneously, we felt like we needed to get some more mass out there and some additional combat power.[34]

Armed with an improved intelligence picture, the leadership of the 3d ACR became even more aware that the solution to the troubles in Al Qaim would require a greater dismounted presence. That would be the role of the reinforcing battalion from the 101st. The availability of this unit, the 3d Battalion, 187th Infantry (3-187 IN), under the command of LTC Joseph Buche, had a significant effect both on the planning and the execution of RIFLES BLITZ. The ground troops from that battalion now became the key element in the clearing of the towns, and their arrival allowed the more mobile troops from the 3d ACR to engage in screening operations.

For the operation, the Tiger Squadron was assigned the mission of manning the border checkpoint and blocking the entire Al Qaim area in order to shut down all movement to and from the towns, with an emphasis around Husaybah. To support this effort, the 3d ACR's Third (or Thunder) Squadron, minus one troop, focused on hemming in Karabilah and Sadah. With the towns isolated, three companies from the 3-187 IN would search every individual structure in the town of Husaybah, while a fourth company would go through the buildings of Karabilah and Sadah. Units from the 3d ACR's Aviation Squadron provided air support, the Support Squadron worked on logistics, an engineer unit helped with the blocking operations, and Special Forces played a key role in shaping and targeting missions. Battery A, 2d Battalion, 5th Field Artillery Regiment, was assigned to provide fire support.[35]

In total, Teeples had the equivalent of three battalions (the bulk of his 1st and 3d Squadrons, a troop from the 2d Squadron and the 3-187 IN battalion) to employ in maneuver roles in RIFLES BLITZ. There was no doubt that such a collection of men and firepower was impressive. To some of the troops of the 3d ACR, the large numbers even looked like overkill. One soldier recalled hearing men say the operation was "like hitting a fly with a sledgehammer."[36] But the numbers of troops and impressive array of firepower could also be misleading. RIFLES BLITZ was not a traditional military combat operation. The emphasis was on noncombat activities. The planners concluded that it was essential to limit the damage in the towns, as overaggressive tactics might further alienate the local population. As Teeples later recalled, "We tried to attain the goal of having the population no worse than neutral toward Coalition forces at the end of the operation."[37]

The 3-187 IN was a good choice for the mission. Since the end of major combat operations in April, the unit's soldiers had focused extensively on working with local populations. The battalion had recruited and trained translators to work with its individual units and had a solid grasp of the standard problems of any counterinsurgency. One of the leaders of the 3d ACR commented on the contributions of the Buche's battalion:

> Obviously the ability to put the number of boots on the ground that they have in an infantry battalion was phenomenal. They had some really sharp company commanders, too, who had been in the thick of things and had been doing urban operations ever since they'd been in country. They brought a bunch of linguists with them that we'd never had the privilege of having down at the levels they were. They had linguists all the way down to the squad levels. LTC Joseph Buche, the battalion commander, even gave up some of his linguists to the other squadrons to help facilitate their efforts. We were just really limited in terms of the linguist capability we have in the regiment as a whole, so that greatly facilitated the interaction with the populace and being able to talk to them. The other thing they brought in was some of their own civil affairs (CA) guys they had embedded with them, which helped us a great deal. They also brought some money in that they had been using up north. They were able to do some things with that money inside Husaybah that facilitated some of the goals and objectives that LTC Buche wanted to accomplish.[38]

Buche had a similar impression of what his unit brought to the area:

> Most of [the 3d ACR's] difficulties in the broader Al Qaim region occurred when they got into the fairly tight villages where most of the people are. It's difficult to move Bradleys in that area,

let alone tanks. To some extent, they'd either been forced to take people who weren't used to operating dismounted and turn them into essentially infantrymen to get them into the center of these areas, or they'd been forced to stay away from the areas where a lot of the people were. The concept of moving through and doing a rigorous and thorough search of every structure in the area was something central to COL Teeples' view of what we needed to do in Husaybah – and to do that he needed a pretty sizable infantry force. That was the rationale he used with MG Swannack, and I presume the same rationale Swannack used with LTG [Ricardo] Sanchez [the Iraq theater commander] in order to get an infantry battalion from somewhere else in theater to assist in the operation.[39]

But the men from the 3-187 IN brought more than just resources and their skills. Members of the battalion had an entirely different mentality from the troopers of the 3d ACR heading into the operation.[40]

The cavalrymen — Tiger Squadron in particular — had been in the towns of the Al Qaim District for months. They had experienced the worst of the insurgent activity and had weathered scores of attacks, all while trying not to alienate the local population with overaggressive tactics. After the long weeks and months in Husaybah and the surrounding area, the soldiers had grown frustrated with the seemingly endless violence and the limited nature of their responses. A journalist recorded how the increased tempo of operations appeared to one enlisted man, "We started off [as] the nice guy. You know, we wanted to come out here. We wanted to help them. We met with a lot of resistance. They attacked us, blew up our vehicles. Everything they could possibly throw at us, they threw at us. And then we pulled out…"[41] A scout in Tiger Squadron had a similar impression: "We tried the passive approach, but that didn't work."[42]

Senior noncommissioned officers felt similarly. 1SG Daniel Hendrex, D Company, wrote in his diary on 13 November: "I am sick of being the hunted. The best defense is an offense, and if you are not proactive in this country, danger seems to creep into your camp."[43]

Buche's troops did not have the same outlook. They were strangers to the area, with little familiarity with the local situation that had frustrated the cavalrymen. In fact, according to Buche, when he first received his orders to participate in RIFLES BLITZ, "It came out of the blue. I'd never heard of Husaybah or Al Qaim, Iraq. When somebody told me that we were headed there, I corrected them the first time and said, 'I think you mean Fallujah.'"[44] Buche noticed the differences in attitude fairly quickly.

He noted that the soldiers of the 3d ACR "had watched their brothers suffer and die and be attacked in this area and we didn't have that perspective. To some extent, then, we were more disposed from the lack of that experience – and from our experience in our AO further north – to interact with the people some more…so that focus on interacting with the people was something we brought there…the lack of the same perspective [as the 3d ACR troopers] actually helped us."[45] One of Buche's officers agreed with this assessment: "We would rather open doors with persuasion than kick them in with our boots."[46] That approach would prove essential in the days to come.

RIFLES BLITZ began in the early hours of 20 November, with predawn raids to capture some of the remaining high-value targets in the towns, especially Husaybah. The raids were by and large successful, picking up dozens of sought-after insurgents, but the success did come at a cost. A HMMWV, part of a small Special Forces convoy moving easterly on Market Street struck an IED. The incident was observed by Tiger Squadron's A Troop, which was positioned at the northeast corner of Husaybah, two blocks east of the police station, searching the nearby *wadi* for insurgents. A Troop's commander, CPT Justin Brown, described what happened next: "… [the special operators were] coming along and just as they get right past the Baath Party headquarters an IED goes off and hits one of their HMMWVs. You could hear the pop and the doors on the backside just blow open. They returned fire towards the Baath Party headquarters."[47] The surviving Special Forces vehicles continued east to Brown's position. The IED explosion had severely wounded one of the operators. Brown's men transported the wounded man to the border checkpoint, past the site of the ambush, where a MEDEVAC helicopter waited. This incident at the start of RIFLES BLITZ was also notable because it was to be the last serious attack on American forces in the entire operation.[48]

Following the predawn raids, Operation RIFLES BLITZ began in earnest. From the very first, it was made clear to the Iraqis in the towns that a sizable force of Americans was now in the area. The commander of the supporting field artillery battery recalled:

> That first day we were just trying to wake [the Iraqis] up and the opening volley was some three-round missions all around the town, very close to the town where the aviation was following up right into it. About that time was when all the phone lines were being cut and the power was being cut. We were just letting them sit there for a while to let them think about what was going on before everything really kicked off.[49]

Indeed roughly half of all the initial field artillery and aviation fire missions were intended to announce the presence of a large American force to the local population, both hostile and otherwise, and was deliberately targeted outside of the towns or on the uninhabited islands in the Euphrates River.[50]

After the artillery and air strikes, the Americans picked up the pace of information operations within the towns. In the months prior to RIFLES BLITZ, Tiger Squadron's information and psychological operations officers had tried to develop a friendly relationship with the local political, community, and business leadership. They took informal polls of the citizens of the towns, established a local television station, and started a program to provide the local population with information on Coalition objectives and activities. The Americans also had a group of translators create a small newspaper that local Iraqis handed out on street corners.[51] On the morning of 20 November, with this information operations structure already in place, the Army began a vigorous campaign to get the word out to the civilian population about the nature of the new operation. Such information operations began at the top, with COL Teeples telling the local mayor and media that "You've got a cancer in your town right now, so we are going to put your community on the operating table. It's going to take a few days, but when we're done…there won't be any more cancer in your community."[52] The statement was the prelude to a more elaborate operation:

> We did do a [leaflet] drop early on as we did the isolation and basically told everybody to stay in their houses and they wouldn't be hurt. We outlined who the folks were that we were looking for, and if they knew anything about them then this is where they could provide information. Really what the leaflet drop did was to explain the purpose of the operation and what the rules were for the residents of the area. Simultaneously to this leaflet drop, we were putting the same message out during Phase 2 on loudspeaker broadcasts. Then as we transitioned into conducting raids, the loudspeaker broadcasts directed the residents not to interfere. The follow-on to that was that the loudspeaker broadcasts provided rules for the citizens and information on the progress of how things were going. We were talking about some of the people who were captured, what they had done, why they were taken in and that sort of thing.[53]

The front of the first leaflet read, in Arabic, "We are here to free your town from the extremists who threaten your future and the future of a free Iraq. If you interfere with the Coalition's hunt for these villains, you may be hurt or killed." It also gave a number the people could call to report criminals and extremists to the Coalition.

The reverse side of the leaflet instructed civilians on the following:

For your safety, follow these rules:

> *Do not enter or leave town without per- mission, you may be killed if you attempt to flee.*
>
> *Have identification ready to prove Iraqi citizenship.*
>
> *A curfew is in effect from dusk to dawn.*
>
> *The coalition will search your home.*
>
> *Bring everyone outside and provide one male to accompany us.*
>
> *Surrender all firearms during searches.*[54]

By using a little ingenuity, the 3-187 IN made its own contribution to the information operations campaign. A lieutenant on the battalion staff proved crucial in building what the unit called "Blues Brothers Mobiles," when, according to LTC Buche, he "went and bought a bunch of mosque loudspeakers, amplifiers and MP3 players," and "figured out a way to hook them up inside vehicles."[55] The operators of these Blues Brothers HMMWVs had about 10 Arabic phrases and those were recorded and placed on the MP3 players. So as a vehicle during a search would move down another block or so, they would play a message that would say, "We come in peace. We're here to search your home. When we come to your door, please meet us with everybody in the home and tell us where any weapons are." One of our information operations (IO) themes that we broadcast as well was, "We're here only as long as we have to be and we'll leave when we've accomplished our mission of ridding Husaybah of enemy personnel."[56]

Buche said that the loudspeaker vehicles, "almost added the equivalent of another interpreter to each force."[57] An officer from the 3d ACR staff later said of the effort, "Given the HMMWVs [the 3-187 IN] had the ability to use those speaker systems and the linguists to communicate, they were pretty effective."[58]

Following the initial raids, field artillery and air strikes, and IO campaign, the soldiers moved in on the ground. In the east, elements from

Thunder Squadron isolated Sadah and Karabilah, cutting off those towns by patrolling and setting up checkpoints along the main highways and in the surrounding countryside. After the squadron surrounded Sadah and Karabilah, one of the 3-187 IN companies cleared Sadah, checking every home while doing so. Thunder Squadron's operations officer described the process: "We went very deliberately through, both mounted and dismounted and with aviation in overwatch, and cleared through the homes from south to north. At the end of the day, if we were halfway through the city, we'd stop and establish security there. We'd secure the area we had cleared, maintain overwatch on the areas we hadn't cleared yet, and then continue on."[59] A sergeant from the 101st remembered, "We were dismounted every day. We cleared every building, every house, every shack, everything, in a systematic manner. We were looking for contraband, weapons, caches and insurgents. There were several characters we were specifically looking for…We cleared from daylight to dark. We then left a platoon in the town to hold onto the bad guys' belt buckle and to make sure that not a whole lot went on under our nose. The next morning, we'd start again."[60] In four days, the Americans cleared more than 500 dwellings in Sadah. Then the infantrymen moved on to Karabilah where the clearing operation followed much the same pattern, moving south to north and searching every dwelling.

The soldiers encountered very little resistance in either town, and in fact, found more significant weapons caches and military facilities in the open areas between the towns and the river. For example, the 3-187 IN's Master SGT Eric Crabtree recalled:

> We did find a pretty good cache along the riverbank and it had what looked like an army surplus store full of equipment. It had about four or five AKs and they were put into the reeds. What the guy had done was to take the pistol grips off the weapons and put them inside these waterproof artillery canisters. He tied strings to them and threw them into the reeds. He also had protective masks, uniforms, and AK pouches. He had enough equipment to outfit a squad. We ended up detaining him and all the males in that area. I remember we took note of one guy who was definitively not Iraqi, perhaps a Syrian or even a Chechen. Our interpreters told us there was no way he was an Iraqi.[61]

The Americans also found and destroyed a buried concrete bunker north of Karabilah. According to Crabtree, the bunker was well constructed, and "This is before Saddam was caught so we figured we were onto something, that we found Saddam. It was definitely a hiding place for somebody, though. We thought we had the golden egg."[62] Unfortunately, that was not the case, but all told, the Americans searched more than 1,000 buildings in the two towns and detained dozens of possible insurgents.

Given its densely populated precincts, Husaybah, the hotbed of the local insurgency, presented a slightly different challenge. Once again, the mobile cavalry troopers from Tiger Squadron cut off the roads, bridges and open areas around the town, preventing anyone from entering or leaving the town. D Company closed down the border checkpoint and, along with a section of A Troop troopers, patrolled and blocked off the built up area of Husaybah.[63] Within the town, however, the close-packed dwellings, the area around the police station, the 440 Block, and crowded Market Street all required special attention. LTC Buche had three infantry companies for the operation, with a reinforced cavalry platoon (two tanks and three Bradleys) from A Troop attached to each. Buche explained how he divided up operations in the town:

> The most experienced of the company commanders was CPT Felix Perez [of D Company, 3-187 IN] who was just an incredible officer. He is very detailed, very specific, and he was really good at considering a number of things and boiling them all down to what was essential. Felix got the southwest part of the town [including the 440 Block] which was probably best suited for his capabilities... Christian Teutsch commanded Charlie Company and his first sergeant was Dave Allard...They were probably my best touchy-feely outfit and we put them in the southeast corner of the town, just based on what we understood and the dynamics we saw at play there...CPT Ed Caracillo [and B Company] was the company commander who had the area around the police station.[64]

In each case, the companies moved west to east, beginning each day at the border checkpoint and advancing at dawn.

But this systematic approach did not mean that the Americans made their tactical routine obvious to the insurgents and the people in the town. The orders to the company commanders stressed the need to be unpredictable: "Change the times you leave and return. Don't always clear in one direction. Mount up, go out the gate, go down the street, and then turn around and come back."[65] Buche explained:

> We hadn't drawn hard lines on the map...What we had done was numbered smaller sectors around town and identified for companies the general area they would be working in. Once a day, we would try and project ahead what sectors to activate. Those were kind of our checkpoints. We would use those to keep

the companies generally clearing, so by the end of the operation we would have cleared and searched the entire town. We also used those to focus the companies on collecting intelligence, patrolling at night, and what we tried to do from time to time was to go back and re-search an area. That way it wouldn't become clear to people that once we searched a building we'd never go back there.[66]

Over the next week or so, the Americans searched and cleared every dwelling in Husaybah, focusing first on the southern section of the town, including the 440 Block. After they cleared that sector, all three companies turned their attention to the crowded and hectic neighborhoods along Market Street. This area greatly concerned the Americans because in the past it had been a known meeting and planning place for the insurgents. In the end, A Troop blocked off the ends of the street, one of the 3-187 IN companies worked its way down the street itself, and the other two covered a two-block area to the north and south. This show of force proved effective — the Americans encountered almost no resistance on Market Street. Indeed, by the end of RIFLES BLITZ on 20 November, Coalition forces had cleared roughly 8,000 dwellings but had engaged in no large firefights and had taken no serious casualties.[67]

Part of the success in avoiding unnecessary bloodshed came from the effort to find a balance between presenting a strong show of force in the cities while not alienating the local population. The orders to the participating units said as much, promising to "dominate our battlespace," while insisting that the troops "conduct all searches in cordial and professional yet thorough manner. Do not cause damage to civilian property unless exceptional circumstances warrant. Do not touch females unless exceptional circumstances warrant."[68] Likewise, on the morning of the first day, Buche decided to risk an ambush by rolling into town with the lights on in their vehicles. He explained, "Part of what I wanted to do was to let any bad guys know that hell was coming to breakfast; that there was a huge force rolling in there." At the same time, he noted, "One of the things we talked about was: what we do today has to make sense tomorrow, next week, next month and next year. While we may be conducting a raid on this one house, there are 20 other homes that are watching what we're doing and what we do has to be explained to them later. Those are the people we have to ensure remain at least neutral to our cause or that whole raid may well be for naught."[69]

The Americans used a number of techniques to maintain favorable relations with the local population, even while they did a thorough, but intrusive, search of the homes. Information operations played a key role. The loudspeakers and television stations announced to the population how the basic search would work. In addition, the soldiers brought leaflets with them to give to each household. Usually at least one of the residents could read. The leaflets explained the process and the temporary suspension of the long-standing rule that allowed each household one AK-47 for self-defense:

> *Please excuse the inconvenience. We must search your home as part of our hunt for the villains who threaten the future of Iraq. We do not want to harm you or your family.*

> *Bring everyone outside and have one man accompany us on the search.*

> *We must collect all weapons. You are not in trouble for having a weapon, but we must collect it at this time. We will announce when the one weapon per home rule is back in effect.*[70]

In addition to communicating with the local population, one of the most important methods for ameliorating the inconvenience to the locals came in the form of money. That is, the Americans gave $20 to every household that cooperated with the search and had no contraband. In addition there was a $40 reward for any tip that led to a weapons cache or targeted insurgent. When the Americans had to break a lock to get into a dwelling or storage area, especially on Market Street, they provided a new lock and set up a system for the owners to retrieve a key from Coalition authorities.[71]

The standard technique for searching courtyards and homes involved sending one squad of men in with two in reserve. According to Master SGT Eric Crabtree, the lead squad "would be as even-tempered and relaxed as the people were. In our company, we'd have the front guy be real talkative and friendly with the people. He'd be with the interpreter and he probably wouldn't hold his weapon in a real aggressive stance, but the guy right behind him would be ready to drop somebody. He was really hyper-vigilant and watched everything that was going on." The search would begin with the interpreter announcing "Hey, we're going to come search your home. Put all the women in one room. We're not going to bother them." Then, Crabtree explained:

> We'd separate all the males. We'd get a good look at their faces, see if they may be somebody of interest, and we'd ask the oldest male of the family to stay with us. We did this so they could see we weren't taking any of their stuff. We'd then systematically search

their home. By that time, we'd learned all the places to look. They stack blankets from the floor to the ceiling, like those Korean mink type blankets. They have hundreds of them, even the poor homes do. We'd search in there for weapons. They'd always have courtyards so we'd search them and look for fresh dirt out there. That's one of the places where we usually found the caches... We systematically cleared the homes. In the summer times, they live on the roofs so you always have to check there as well. We tried to be respectful and get somebody from the home involved so they understood we weren't there to rob them, which is what they automatically think...Once they were compliant, they only had one AK and didn't give us any problems, we'd thank them and give them the $20 and be on our way.[72]

One embedded reporter described the inevitable tension during one such search, "The young soldiers enter people's compounds with a mix of menace and apprehension. As they march in, gripping their weapons, they awkwardly tell the inhabitants 'Peace be with you' in broken Arabic. Young girls nervously watch Americans prod through their household belongings. Old men act as if they have seen it all before."[73]

For ten days, from dawn till dusk, the Americans repeated the process, searching some 8,000 individual structures, handing out $20 to compliant households, arresting nearly 400 suspected insurgents, and confiscating hundreds of weapons. The operation did suffer some setbacks, and the soldiers did make mistakes. For example, RIFLES BLITZ coincided with the Eid al-Fitr festival that ended the Islamic holy month of Ramadan. Some of the local celebrations caused friction. At one point, Buche had to contact the mayor of Husaybah to warn him to tell the local children to stop shooting toy guns near American soldiers.[74] In addition, several observers worried that the local population would be traumatized by the operations, and that the trauma would create more opposition to the Americans.[75] Some disgruntled local citizens backed up that concern, such as the individuals who had been outside of the towns when the operation began and could not return until it ended. One such man complained to a reporter, "They... say they want to bring us freedom and happiness but instead they are just making enemies out of every one of us."[76] Even the mayor of Husaybah expressed some concern; "Of course, there is action and there is reaction. This is my opinion and many people are arrested. Many families have lost a son. Some people have been killed by mistake."[77]

In the short term, however, there was very little evidence that such concerns came to fruition. The Americans certainly felt that they received a generally positive reception from the local population. The operations officer for the 3d ACR recalled:

> I think for the most part the civilians who didn't have anything to hide were pretty appreciative of us coming in there. They'd been suffering pretty hard at the hands of these guys strong arming them inside the towns…If the house was good to go, if the people were cooperative and weren't hiding anything and basically they did everything we asked them to, we gave them $20 for their trouble. We had a pot of money we could use how we saw fit, and that was one way we saw for putting money in the people's hands and to say, "Thank you for supporting us." Word got out pretty quick and everyone was trying to be nice and everything, but they couldn't get out there quick enough to dig up the caches that were in their backyards. I'd say that for the most part, the people who were just trying to do their day-to-day thing, live their lives and weren't a part of the folks who were causing the problems in the town were very happy we were there.[78]

Another officer said of RIFLES BLITZ, "The $20, it sounds really hokey, but I think it is starting to sway the people, and the presence of the soldiers and the way the soldiers are conducting it. In fact, down here, the soldiers got invited in for tea and crumpets. That is a good thing, because we will get some intel[ligence] out of those guys."[79] A platoon leader who had been on the ground in Husaybah during the worst of the violence maintained, "When we show up like this with 3,500 soldiers, it shows the local people that it is OK for them to show us where the bad guys are, and they don't have to be afraid of those people."[80] One troop commander put it slightly differently, "Iraqis will defer to whichever authority shows the greatest strength. If the insurgents look like they were in charge of an area/city and US forces appeared weak, then the locals will defer to the insurgents and be against US forces. If US forces acted decisively, then they would support US forces, and be against the insurgents. Iraq is a 'might-makes-right' society."[81]

These officers proved prescient. A businessman in Husaybah worried that his company had suffered during the operation, telling one reporter, "We desperately want our freedom back but we are happy to cooperate with the Americans if they can bring us peace."[82] The Americans' experiences matched this statement, "In a lot of cases, as we went through the houses we constantly got tips from the locals on who the people were that were causing the problems…Because of the way we were treating the people, they were really offering up a lot of information."[83] The trend continued after RIFLES BLITZ ended, when the Americans saw a clear increase in the numbers of informants, including the 14-year-old son of an insurgent leader who risked his life to turn in his father and other prominent members of the insurgency.[84] The Americans could also sense a generally more positive attitude from the local population. One officer remembered that after RIFLE BLITZ, "you could tell just by how they were looking and waving at us, some people thanking us as we were going by. They appreciated what we were doing in town and were integral to our success."[85] Another participant recalled that afterwards, "for the last three months I was there, the Iraqis threw us a feast every single Thursday…The craziest one of all was at Christmas time when the Iraqis brought us a pig and roasted it over a stick. It's against their religion, but they did it because they thought Americans liked pig. That just sticks in my mind that a lot of them were starting to lead better lives and that this mattered to them."[86]

Perhaps most telling of all about the success of TIGER STRIKE, ALL AMERICAN TIGER, the removal of Mowhoush, the efforts of D Company, and RIFLES BLITZ was the complete cessation of all insurgent activity in the Al Qaim District for more than a month. As one officer recalled, "what became evident was [that] things became real quiet, real quick in that town."[87] Reilly agreed, "As a result of this operation we did not experience a single act of violence in six weeks, within the entire area, following the operation. I have never seen this type of result anywhere in Iraq, previous or since this operation."[88] The 3d ACR also received funding in the aftermath of RIFLES BLITZ to rebuild infrastructure, build schools, improve wells, and create jobs, all of which only endeared them more to the local population.[89] At the same time, the regiment accelerated its efforts to turn border security over to newly trained Iraqi forces, and by the new year the Iraqis began to move into position.

The first new insurgent activity in Husaybah came on Christmas Day, with a mortar attack on the border checkpoint. The attacks slowly increased in January and February 2004, but never approached the violence of September and October. By March and April, the Al Qaim District ceased to be the concern of the 3d ACR, as the regiment handed off the region to a Marine battalion. Some of the Marines believed that the soldiers had been too heavy-handed with the local population, and most of the soldiers worried that the Marines did not have enough armor, but overall the transition went smoothly.[90] Within months the Marines had their own troubles in the district, but that is a different story. In the late fall of 2003, even as they discovered just how difficult the war was going to be, the soldiers in the Al Qaim District managed to adjust on the fly and bring peace, however fleeting, to one of the formerly most violent regions of Iraq.

Notes

1. COL David Teeples, interview by Peter Connors, 4 November 2005, Washington, DC; MAJ James Gallivan, interview by the author, 6 September 2006, Fort Leavenworth.

2. Quoted in Bay Fang and Bruce B. Auster, "Iraq: A Magnet for Angry, Fervent Men," *US News and World Report* 135 (29 September 2003): 18.

3. LTC Paul Calvert, interview by John McCool, 17 February 2006, Fort Leavenworth (hereafter Calvert Interview 1); LTC Paul Calvert, interview by the author, 14 September 2006, Fort Leavenworth (hereafter Calvert Interview 2).

4. Teeples Interview; Raymond Bonner, "For G.I.'s in Isolated Town, Unknown Enemy is Elusive," *New York Times* (21 October 2003): A12.

5. MAJ Justin Brown, interview by the author, 7 September 2006, Fort Leavenworth.

6. Teeples interview.

7. Calvert Interview 2; A number of other smaller units were attached to the 82nd Airborne and to 3rd ACR in the summer and early fall of 2003, but not enough to change the basic calculus at the time. For more detail on the breakdown of the units see Teeples interview; LTC Gregory D. Reilly, email interview with Lynne Garcia, Combat Studies Institute, 30 May 2006, Fort Leavenworth (hereafter Reilly interview 1); LTC Gregory D. Reilly, email interview by the author, 15 September 2006, Fort Leavenworth (hereafter Reilly Interview 2); MAJ Vincent Torza, interview by the author, 15 September 2006, Fort Leavenworth; MAJ Thomas Neemeyer, interview by John McCool, 2 December 2005, Fort Leavenworth.

8. Reilly interview 1-2. .

9. Fang and Auster, "Iraq: A Magnet," 18.

10. LTC Gregory Reilly, journal, 10 October; CPT Daniel Ruecking, interview by the author, 13 October 2006, Fort Leavenworth; Stephen J. Hedges, "US Forces Step Up Patrols, Raids on Homes in Iraq," *Knight Ridder Tribune Business News*, (22 October 2003), 1.

11. Reilly journal, Emphasis in original.

12. Reilly journal.

13. Reilly journal.

14. 1LT Shannon Thompson quoted in Chuck D. Meseke, "Operation Rifles Blitz: 'Bandit Troop' Goes on the Offensive," *Defend America News*, 2 December 2003, online at <http://www.defendamerica.mil>, accessed 22 August 2006.

15. Calvert interview 2.

16. Reilly interview 2.

17. Daniel Hendrex, *A Soldier's Promise: The Heroic True Story of an*

American Soldier and an Iraqi Boy (New York: Simon Spotlight, 2006), 93.

18. Patrick J. McDonnell, "Coalition Gains Insight Into Iraq's Foreign Insurgents," *Los Angeles Times*, 9 February 2004, 1; Alexander Trudeau, "The Jihad Superbowl," *Macleans.ca*, 8 December 2003, online at <http://www. macleans. ca>, accessed 22 August 2006.

19. Hedges, "US Forces," 1.

20. Calvert interview 2.

21. For a negative depiction of TIGER STRIKE, see Rosen's four-part article, "Every Time the Wind Blows," *Asia Times*, 24-30 October 2003, online at <http://www.atimes.com>, accessed 12 September 2006.

22. Brown interview; Josh White, "Documents Tell of Brutal Improvisation by GIs," *Washington Post*, 3 August 2005, A1. See also Alfred W. McCoy, *A Question of Torture: CIA Interrogation from the Cold War to the War on Terror* (New York: Metropolitan Boos, 2006), 144-145.

23. Calvert interview, 18.

24. CPT Terrence Buckeye, email interview by author, 12 September 2006, Fort Leavenworth.

25. CPT Chad Roehrman, interview by the author, 18 October 2006, Fort Leavenworth.

26. Roehrman interview

27. Master SGT Daniel Hendrex, interview by the author, 14 September 2006, Fort Leavenworth. Another description is found in Hendrex, *Soldiers Promise*, 100- 108; Reilly journal, 10 November 2003; and "11 November Ambush Narrative," in author's possession, provided by Master SGT Daniel Hendrex.

28. "40 Rounds Later...Observations of Dragon (Heavy) Company," unpublished manuscript in author's possession, provided by Master SGT Daniel Hendrex. See also Roehrman interview, Hendrex interview, and Hendrex, *Soldier's Promise*, 97-98.

29. Roehrman interview. See also Hendrex, *Soldier's Promise*, 110.

30. Hendrex interview; Hendrex, *Soldier's Promise*, 109-115; Roehrman interview; Reilly journal, 15 November 2003.

31. Reilly journal.

32. Calvert interview, 19-20.

33. Reilly interview 2.

34. Calvert interview 2.

35. Teeples interview, 8, 21.

36. Hendrex, *Soldier's Promise*, 127.

37. Quoted in Tom Roeder, "Carson Troops Used Cash for Cooperation During Stint in Iraq," *Colorado Springs Gazette*, 9 April 2004: A1.

38. Calvert interview 2.

39. Buche interview.

40. By all accounts, the combination of the two units went smoothly, no doubt helped by the fact that several of the leaders were friends from earlier assignments in the Army. In the case of Reilly and Buche, they had attended the School of Advanced Military Studies together. See especially Buche interview, Reilly interview, Calvert interview, Brown interview, and Crabtree interview.

41. SPC Alan Caldwell quoted in "Profile: Operation by 3d Armored Cavalry Regiment Along the Iraqi-Syrian Border," Transcript, *All Things Considered*, National Public Radio, 24 November 2003.

42. PFC Carl Roush quoted in Meseke, "Operation Rifles Blitz."

43. Hendrex, *Soldier's Promise*, 109.

44. Buche interview.

45. Buche interview.

46. MAJ Robert Dees quoted in Philip Smucker, "US Hunts Rebels One City at a Time," *Washington Times*, (27 November 2003), A13.

47. Brown interview.

48. Brown interview.

49. CPT Anthony Yeatts, interview by the author, 7 September 2006, Fort Leavenworth.

50. Yeatts interview; Roeder, "Carson Troops." Most of the other fire missions were for illumination.

51. Ruecking interview.

52. Quoted in Bay Fang, "Getting Offensive," *US News and World Report*, 8 December 2003, online at <http://www.usnews.com>, accessed 21 August 2006.

53. Calvert interview 2.

54. "1/3 ACR OPORD 03-40 (OPERATION TIGER BLITZ)," 16 November 2003, in author's possession.

55. Buche interview.

56. Buche interview.

57. Buche interview.

58. Calvert interview 2.

59. Gallivan interview.

60. Master SGT Eric Crabtree, interview by author, 16 October 2006, Fort Leavenworth.

61. Crabtree interview.

62. Crabtree interview.

63. Roehrman interview; Brown interview; "1/3 ACR OPORD 03-40."

64. Buche interview.

65. "Iron Hammer Explanation," LTC Joseph Buche, n.d., in author's possession..

66. Buche interview.

67. Brown interview; Teeples Interview: Reilly interview 2; Calvert interview; Buche interview.

68. "1/3 ACR OPORD 03-40."

69. Buche interview.

70. "1/3 ACR OPORD 03-40."

71. Brown interview; Buche interview; Roehrman interview.

72. Crabtree Interview.

73. Trudeau, "Jihad Superbowl."

74. Smucker, "US Hunts," A13. Buche later said that he probably overreacted, see Buche interview.

75. For example James Hider wrote in the *London Times*, "As soldiers swept the town of cinderblock one-storey houses, occasionally kicking down doors not opened voluntarily, groups of sullen Iraqis lined the streets to stare. Some responded to the waves from the lorry loads of soldiers in full combat gear, most just glared impassively back." "US Forces Unleashed on Border Town Rebels," *London Times*, (21 November 2003): 24. See also "Profile: Operation by 3d Armored Cavalry Regiment Along the Iraqi-Syrian Border;" Trudeau, "Jihad Superbowl."

76. Quoted in Fang, "Getting Offensive."

77. Quoted in Philip Smucker, "US Launches New Anti-Insurgent Operation Near Syrian Border," *Voice of America News*, 28 November 2003, online at http://www.voanews.com, accessed 27 September 2006.

78. Calvert Interview 2.

79. Quoted in Smucker, "US Launches."

80. 1LT Shannon Thompson quoted in Meseke, "Operation Rifles Blitz."

81. Buckeye interview. A similar sentiment could be found in many of the recollections of the fight. See also the SPC Alan Caldwell quotation in, "Profile: Operation by 3d Armored Cavalry Regiment Along the Iraqi-Syrian Border."

82. Quoted in "US Officers Play Down the Role of Foreign Fighters in Attacks on Them," *Irish Times*, (25 November 2003), 11.

83. Calvert interview 2.

84. On the increase in informants, see Reilly interview 2; Calvert interview 2; Torza interview; and Hendrex interview. On the boy, see Hendrex interview; Hendrex, *Soldier's Promise*, passim; and Sudarsan Raghavan, "Son of Iraqi Guerrilla Leader Becomes Major US Intelligence Resource," *Knight Ridder Tribune Business News*, 17 December 2003: 1.

85. Roehrman interview.

86. Yeatts interview.

87. Calvert interview 1.

88. Reilly interview 1.

89. Brown interview; Calvert interview 2.

90. Reilly interview 1; Brown interview; Roehrman interview; Torza interview; Hendrex interview.

A Brigade Replaces a Division
Northern Iraq, January 2004

by

John J. McGrath

In early 2004, the bulk of the troops participating in the original Operation IRAQI FREEDOM (OIF-I) rotation were replaced by units of the second rotation (OIF-II). During this transition, the roughly 25,000 troops assigned or attached to the 101st Airborne Division (Air Assault), which had been responsible for security in northern Iraq, were replaced by a force of about 10,000 troops assigned or attached to a newly created headquarters called Task Force *Olympia* (TFO). TFO was built around the 3d Brigade, 2d Infantry Division, which was the US Army's first Stryker brigade. Prior to this unit turnover, northern Iraq had been one of the least-restive areas of the country, despite its mix of Sunni Arab, Kurd, and Christian and Turkman groups. This relatively calm environment was the rationale for troop downsizing, along with the belief that a Stryker brigade brought increased capabilities over other kinds of brigades and that the nascent Iraqi Security Forces would play an increased role in the security of the area.[1] Once the decision was made for a reduced deployment, Task Force Olympia commander BG Carter Ham, and 3d Brigade commander, COL Michael Bounds, had to develop plans to deploy this reduced force throughout their area of operations (AO) without losing the momentum and effectiveness displayed by the 101st during its tenure. Additionally, these commanders had to respond to a changing situation during their deployment by moving forces around to critical points, request and integrate reinforcements, and respond to requests from higher headquarters to detach task force units for use in theater-level missions.

The northern Iraq area of operations consisted of the provinces of Nineveh, Dahuk, Arbil and Sulaymaniyah. Dahuk, Arbil, and Sulaymaniyah provinces in the north and northeast are Kurdish. Almost all of the land area of these mountainous provinces was behind the Green Line, the longstanding demarcation between autonomous Kurdistan and the rest of Iraq. Accordingly, the Kurdish provinces required minimal occupation forces. Most of the US effort in Dahuk and Arbil and Sulaymaniyah involved guarding the border and providing reconstruction support.[2]

Nineveh Province, in the northwest, was a different story. The province stretched over 13,861 square miles (137 by 165 miles) from Kurdistan to the Syrian border. With an estimated population of 2.4 million in 2004, the province had a population density of 173.2 inhabitants per square mile.[3]

The bulk of the provincial population was centered on the valley of the Tigris River, which ran generally in a north-south direction through the eastern portion of the province. Almost two thirds of this population (1.7 million) lived in the sprawling city of Mosul on the banks of the Tigris, making the city and its environs the most important area of Nineveh. In general, the population in Nineveh was predominantly Kurdish east of the Tigris and predominantly Sunni-Arab west of the river. This held true in Mosul as well. In addition to Kurds and Sunni-Arabs, the province also contained sizeable minorities of Christian and Turkman groups. The city of Tal Afar, about 50 miles west of Mosul, was a Turkman city. Its location near the Syrian border made it a key location, particularly when foreign fighters would later join the insurgency. There were other important areas aside from Mosul and Tal Afar. South of Mosul, along the Tigris, was a Sunni heartland as potent to the insurgency as the famous Sunni Triangle in central Iraq. At the southern end of this region were the city of Qayyarah and the large airbase complex known as Q-West. Q-West was important not only as a military hub for the area, but also because of its proximity to the Iraq-Turkey oil pipeline.

The oil industry and its associated infrastructure were important to northern Iraq. The Iraq-Turkey pipeline ran parallel to the Tigris through the heavy Sunni region south of Mosul and in the area between Mosul and Tal Afar north to Turkey. This pipeline primarily brought oil from the large oilfield that extended from southeast of Mosul in Arbil Province to northwest of the city of Kirkuk in Tamim Province. Pipeline protection was a vital mission. Mosul had a large oil refinery and the administrative infrastructure for the Northern Oil Company, a major component of the nationalized Iraqi Oil Company. In addition to oil pipelines, electric power lines were key elements of infrastructure in Nineveh. Northwest of Mosul, the Tigris was dammed at Daw al Qamar, forming a large reservoir and power plant with the capability to provide hydroelectric power to a large part of the country if the operation of the plant and the power lines were not disrupted.

The road network in northern Iraq was also important to any US force operating there. Since this part of Iraq was the farthest from the ports of the Persian Gulf, the main roads from the south, National Routes 1 and 2, were also main supply routes (MSR) that had to be maintained and kept open. Route1, known as MSR TAMPA south of Mosul, was the main north- south route in Iraq. This route ran north from Baghdad to Mosul, traveling generally slightly to the west of the Tigris River. Route 2, known as MSR SANTA FE south of Mosul, followed a more easterly course, running from Kirkuk through Arbil and then on to Mosul east of the Tigris. North of the Tigris, Route 2 became MSR TAMPA and traveled north to a key border crossing with Turkey in Dahuk Province. Route 1, known as MSR SANTA FE north of Mosul, ran to the northeast to the Syrian border. A vital secondary road, Route 47, branched off Route 1 north of Mosul and extended to the west, through Tal Afar and the town of Sinjar to the Syrian border.

The 101st Airborne Division (Air Assault) arrived in the Mosul area in late April 2003 after participating in battles in the southern Iraqi cities of Najaf, Karbala and Hillah, and after garrisoning part of Baghdad for several weeks. Northern Iraq had not participated in any of the major fighting of March and April 2004. Subsequently the Iraqi forces there voluntarily surrendered to a small force of US Marines, Army Special Forces troops and Kurdish militia. The 101st, commanded by MG David Petraeus, moved into a governmental vacuum in northern Iraq. There looting and lawlessness was rampant to the point that the small Marine force had moved to the large airfield in southwestern Mosul and remained there awaiting reinforcement. When the 2d Brigade arrived at the airfield, it expected to have to fight its way into Mosul, but its subordinate units were able to move into the city without violence and occupy their assigned sectors.[4]

The 101st was the largest division in the US Army in 2004. In addition to the standard division elements, including three maneuver brigades of three infantry battalions each, the division also contained two aviation brigades: an attack brigade equipped with AH-64 Apache attack helicopters; and an assault brigade, equipped with UH-60 Blackhawk and CH-47 Chinook transportation helicopters. These helicopters gave the division a unique source of readily available aerial mobility and firepower. Logistically, the division was augmented with a corps support group in addition to its own extensive support elements. Additional augmentations included an engineer group, a civil affairs battalion, a psychological operations company and a long range surveillance company. The total force was roughly 25,000 soldiers, which provided a troop density of about 10.41 troops per thousand of population.[5]

Once the dust settled in the 101st Airborne Division's redeployment to northern Iraq, troop deployment within Nineveh Province was divided primarily between the division's three maneuver brigades with attached units. The 2d Brigade, commanded by COL Joseph Anderson, remained in

Mosul, while COL Benjamin Hodges's 1st Brigade operated out of Q-West. The 3d Brigade, under COL Michael Linnington, was based out of a large airfield complex southwest of Tal Afar. Division troops, including most of the Division Support Command, the Division Artillery headquarters and the division headquarters, were in Mosul. The division aviation assets were primarily split between the airfields at Mosul, Q-West and Tal Afar.

Anderson's 2d Brigade operated primarily out of the Mosul airfield complex, which also included a large former Baathist military cantonment just west of the airport. Anderson deployed four infantry battalions and one field artillery battalion in Mosul conducting counterinsurgency and stability operations. Elements from the division headquarters and support command, located nearby, provided direct support to the 2d Brigade.[6]

The 1st Brigade was organized as a combat team working out of the Q-West airfield. The brigade was responsible for a large sector which included the Tigris valley insurgent heartland, a long stretch of the Iraq-Turkey pipeline and a large ammunition dump near the old Parthian city of Hatra. The division's 101st Assault Aviation Brigade, commanded by COL Gregory Gass, also was based out of Q-West, although its attack helicopter battalions and air cavalry squadron were able to range the whole divisional sector, providing security and reconnaissance to support division operations. A portion of one of the attack battalions supported the 4th Infantry Division to the south, working out of Kirkuk, while one battalion (3-101st Aviation) was placed under the 1st Brigade and given its own area of operations east of the Tigris.[7]

The 101st's 3d Brigade was a combat team operating from the Tal Afar airfield complex outside that city. COL Linnington's forces were not only responsible for Tal Afar, but also the Syrian border extending south of the Tigris down to Anbar Province. The brigade headquarters, direct support field artillery battalion and the brigade support troops operated directly out of the Tal Afar airfield. The field artillery battalion guarded oil refinery sites and provided security for oil tanker convoys coming out of Syria. Each of the three infantry battalions had large sectors.

The 1-187th Infantry (1-187 IN) had a sector northwest of and in the city of Tal Afar. The 2-187th Infantry (2-187 IN) operated west of Tal Afar centered on the town of Sinjar. This sector included 89 towns and villages, with an estimated population of 200,000. It also included more than 70 miles of Syrian border along with the high ground known as Sinjar Mountain, which overlooked the border and was a key observation and

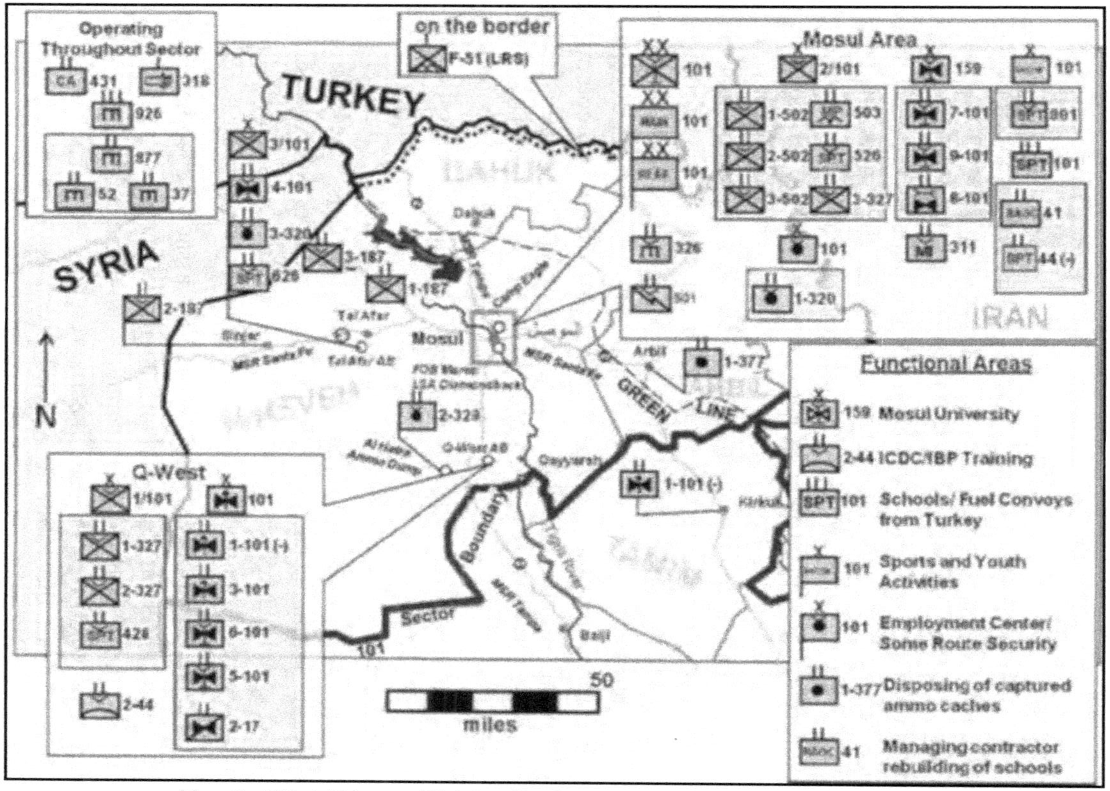

Map 8. 101st Airborne Division Deployment, Northern Iraq, 2003-2004.

communications post. North of the 2-187, the 3-187th Infantry (3-187 IN) had a sector along the Syrian border northwest of Tal Afar. In November2003, this battalion was temporarily shifted south into Anbar Province to provide infantry support for the 3d Armored Cavalry Regiment that operated in cities along the Euphrates River near the Syrian border.[8]

Petraeus's division contained many elements important and useful in a high- or mid-intensity battle, but which became somewhat superfluous in a low-intensity counterinsurgency fight. The ever-resourceful division commander employed these headquarters and units in various functions related to stability operations. While some of these missions related directly to combat operations, some did not. The attached corps support group was tasked with providing route or convoy security for fuel convoys traveling down Route 2 from Turkey along with overseeing the restoration of the provincial school system. One of the group's subordinate units, the 41st Rear Area Operations Center, was in charge of restoring local schools. The Division Support Command headquarters ran the youth and sports commission. The divisional signal battalion used its expertise to restore the civil communications infrastructure. While still coordinating division fire support and conducting convoy security operations and small projects in villages near Mosul, the Division Artillery headquarters primarily focused on establishing and running the Veteran's Employment Office in the city. An attached field artillery battalion was responsible for disposing of large caches of captured ammunition in Kurdistan. Aside from its organic engineer battalion, the 101st also had an engineer group, providing the division with four engineer battalions. These engineers were readily available assets to conduct public works and reconstruction projects throughout northern Iraq. Throughout the 101st's tour of duty, the engineers were constantly employed on such missions.[9]

The 159th Aviation Brigade, the 101st's assault helicopter brigade, had its headquarters at the Mosul airfield, but its battalions were scattered throughout the division's area to support the maneuver brigades, provide transportation, patrol, and perform aerial resupply missions. Petraeus and his staff assigned the 159th headquarters with the mission of reopening Mosul's large university. This monumental task was soon accomplished, with final exams for the disrupted spring 2003 term actually being held in the summer.[10]

Another 101st initiative was the early creation of Iraqi-manned security forces and the restoration of the local police. The divisional air defense battalion, the 2d Battalion, 44th Air Defense Artillery (2-44th

ADA), commanded by LTC Donald Fryc, had this mission. In early June 2003, Fryc's battalion created the Joint Iraqi Security Company (JISC) in Mosul, a force recruited from all local ethnic groups. In July, the JISC, with a dual US-Iraqi chain of command, was integrated into the security force guarding the base in Mosul where the division headquarters was located. With the reestablishment of the Iraqi Border Police (IBP) and the creation of the Iraqi Civil Defense Corps (ICDC), the 2-44th ADA assumed the role of the primary trainer. The battalion initially provided basic training at the Mosul airfield (specifically at the portion of the cantonment known as Camp Claiborne) but eventually established a large training facility at Q-West. The ICDC and IBP started as company-level units, but were eventually expanded into battalion-sized units. While the ADA battalion took the lead in this area, other units assisted in their areas of responsibility, particularly in reestablishing the local police. For example, the 2-187 IN (based in Sinjar) trained an 800-man police force and 300-man border guard unit. On Iraqi Army Day, 6 January 2004, two ICDC battalions and one Border Police battalion were activated in Mosul. This completed the organization of four ICDC and three IBP battalions in northern Iraq during the tour of the 101st Airborne Division in northern Iraq in 2003 and 2004.[11]

During its tour of duty in northern Iraq, the 101st used its force of roughly 25,000 to maximum advantage in both counterinsurgency and stability operations. The mobility and firepower provided by the division's large fleet of helicopters aided these operations. The availability of divisional and attached units to focus on specific aspects of stability operations allowed the division to make great progress in restoring the infrastructure of Nineveh Province. While other parts of Iraq, specifically Baghdad, Anbar, and Najaf, seemed on the verge of insurgent-induced chaos, northern Iraq, despite its volatile mix of ethnic groups, was calm in early 2004 when the 101st began making preparations to return to its home station at Fort Campbell, Kentucky.

From the start, the Department of Defense (DOD) planned to execute a unit rotation scheme for the units deployed to Operation IRAQI FREEDOM, starting with the ones which participated in the Baghdad campaign. As a prelude to this, the Marine forces that had been garrisoning a large section of southern Iraq and the 3d Infantry Division (Mechanized) had been withdrawn in September 2003. As early as July 2003, GEN Jack Keane, the Army Vice Chief of Staff, announced the rotation plan which was referred to as Operation IRAQI FREEDOM II (OIF II). In reference to the 101st Airborne Division, Keane commented that the current plan was to replace the division with a yet to be determined multinational division.[12]

As late as October 2003, less than four months before the 101st's projected departure, replacement details were not firm. DOD was still planning for the deployment of a multinational division in northern Iraq, preferably made up of troops from Islamic countries but, with no arrangements in place, Defense Secretary (SECDEF) Donald Rumsfeld commented that a different solution, a back-up plan for using American forces, would be implemented if necessary. It would be up to LTG Ricardo Sanchez, the commander of the Combined Joint Task Force-7 (CJTF-7), the theater command in Iraq, and the Army Chief of Staff, GEN Peter Schoomaker, to come up with an alternate deployment solution.[13]

With the available resources of the US Army at their disposal, Sanchez and Schoomaker had several options for replacing the 101st with US troops.[14] The first option was to assemble a division's worth of troops from the assets of the Army worldwide. A second option would be to extend the 101st in Iraq until additional troops were ready to replace them. A third option would be a realignment of the divisions in Iraq in order to cover northern Iraq with a division moved from somewhere else in the country. A fourth option would be to replace the air-assault division with a smaller unit, a brigade, preferably one with enhanced firepower and mobility, making this option an economy-of-force operation. The brigade could be selected from the Army as a whole or from the redistribution of units already in Iraq.

The advantages of deploying a full replacement division for the 101st would be that the new unit would be a roughly equivalent-sized force. This would cause minimal disruption in the stability and counterinsurgency effort in northern Iraq. However, there were disadvantages to deploying a division in early 2004. At that time, the Army consisted of ten division headquarters in the active component and eight in the Army National Guard (ARNG). Of these 18 commands, seven either had just returned from deployments or were about to do so. An additional three were already scheduled to deploy to specific areas in Iraq and Afghanistan. Seven division headquarters were composed completely of ARNG units, which would require a certain amount of post-mobilization preparation before they could deploy. By fall 2003, it was already too late to mobilize and prepare these units in time to get them to replace the 101st in early 2004. The one remaining division headquarters was that of the 2d Infantry, which had been stationed in Korea since 1965. Since that time, no US forces had ever been temporarily deployed out of Korea. The 2d Division headquarters was integrated into the defense of South Korea at a time when North Korea was becoming increasingly bellicose. Shifting the 2d's headquarters would probably be viewed as a move of desperation.[15]

A division headquarters would require three subordinate maneuver brigades to duplicate the 101st's trace on the ground. In early 2004, the Army consisted of 73 brigades or their equivalent, with 34 in the active component and 39 in the ARNG. Of the ARNG brigades, 29 were in a pre-mobilization state and, therefore, not available. In early 2004, 15 brigades were deployed or pending deployment, 22 brigades had just completed deployment, and five brigades were either preparing for deployment or training to become a Stryker unit. Therefore, of the 73 existing brigades, 70 were unavailable to staff a proposed division. The remaining three brigade equivalents were the 1st Brigade and 2d Brigade, 2d Infantry Division, in Korea, and the 11th Armored Cavalry Regiment at Fort Irwin, California. The deployment of each of these units to Iraq was problematic. Similar to the problems associated with the deployment of the 2d Infantry Division headquarters, the division's 1st and 2d brigades were tied into the defense of South Korea and had been continuously stationed in that country since 1965. While the brigades could theoretically be used, their sudden departure from Korea could be viewed with greater importance than the action actually represented. The third brigade-sized unit was the 11th Armored Cavalry Regiment (ACR), which served as the OPFOR (Opposing Forces) unit at the National Training Center (NTC). As such, the ACR had a special organization and a key ongoing training mission.[16]

The 101st could be extended in Iraq until ARNG units could be mobilized or the 11th ACR and/or 2d Infantry Division could be prepared. Throughout the OIF deployments, some divisions and brigades were extended for several months in Iraq. For example, the 1st Armored Division would have several units extended during the OIFI/OIFII transition but resorting to such extensions was only to be used to respond to increased insurgent activity. The 1st Armored Division had been extended when Shiite extremists seized areas of Baghdad, Najaf, Karbala, and Hillah. The troops were used to defeat these insurgents. In contrast, northern Iraq was relatively calm in early 2004.

The one advantage to keeping the 101st would be continuity in northern Iraq. However, such an extension also would have many disadvantages. Primarily, it would violate the policy of sending home, as soon as possible, the troops who had participated in the 2003 Baghdad campaign. The 101st had fought in the cities of Najaf, Karbala, and Hillah in March and April 2003. An extension would also be a reversal of public statements made by

DOD and Army officials. In October 2003, SECDEF Rumsfeld had clearly stated that the 101st would be replaced.[17]

Sanchez could shift divisions within the theater so that northern Iraq would be covered by a unit already in the theater. While this option solved the problem of replacing the 101st, it would also create new ones. As pointed out above, almost every available division and brigade was already deployed. A shifting of divisions would result in fewer troops in volatile areas of Iraq, such as Baghdad, the Sunni Triangle, and the enflamed Shiite areas south of Baghdad. Northern Iraq would probably remain under control, but these other areas would then be even more restive than they already were. Moving large units around could create unnecessary holes.

Instead of replacing the 101st with a division, however, Sanchez could turn northern Iraq into an economy-of-force operation and replace it with a reinforced brigade. While there were few available brigades outside of Iraq, there were several in theater that could possibly fit the bill. In particular, the first of the new Stryker brigades, the 3d Brigade, 2d Infantry Division, had arrived in October 2003 and had been attached to the 4th Infantry Division (Mechanized) operating out of Samarra at the northern part of the Sunni Triangle. Although just a brigade in size, using the Stryker unit had certain advantages. The Strykers provided tactical mobility, firepower and armored protection that could prove useful in a city like Mosul. Additionally, the brigade contained three infantry battalions, an anti-armor company, a field artillery battalion and a cavalry squadron, making it larger than most other brigades. Sophisticated digital communications equipment allowed Stryker unit commanders to effectively communicate and maintain a high level of situational awareness. If any brigade in the Army could take over a divisional sector, the Stryker brigade was the unit.[18]

There were other reasons for turning northern Iraq into an economy-of-force operation. Under the 101st, Nineveh Province and the adjoining Kurdish area seemed to be well on their way to stability and reconstruction. In addition, 10,000 Iraqi Security Force (ISF) troops were now trained. Apart from city police, these forces included four freshly raised and trained ICDC and three IBP battalions. These local forces were available to augment the US brigade. Since September, Petraeus had been slowly pulling back 101st units, handing over more authority to the local Iraqi government apparatus. Replacing the division with a brigade would, therefore, be just a continuation of this policy.[19]

With the inability to gain support for forming a multinational division in northern Iraq, Sanchez had to decide whether to press for additional troops, which were not readily available, or to shuffle his own forces around. Using his own forces, Sanchez could either keep a division in the north and provide less coverage elsewhere, or he could turn Nineveh into an economy-of-force province, replacing the division with a brigade.

US planners chose to replace the 101st Airborne Division (Air Assault) with the reinforced brigade-sized Stryker force. The northern AO was slightly reduced by transferring responsibility for the easternmost Kurdish province, Sulaymaniyah, to the 4th Infantry Division (Mechanized). Replacing the 101st's large headquarters would be a smaller, newly created, ad hoc headquarters. In December 2003, Army Chief of Staff Schoomaker tasked the I Corps, at Fort Lewis, Washington, with this requirement. The I Corps commander, LTG Edward Soriano, tasked his Deputy Commander for Training and Readiness, BG Carter Ham, with forming and commanding the new headquarters, designated Task Force *Olympia*. Ham had been in his position since August 2003 and had overseen the deployment of the first Stryker Brigade (3d Brigade, 2d Infantry Division) from Fort Lewis to Samarra, Iraq. This brigade, after being shifted to Mosul, would form the bulk of the.[20]

The 3d Brigade, with three infantry battalions, a cavalry squadron, field artillery battalion, anti-armor company, and military intelligence company, provided the bulk of the TFO but it also had an air cavalry squadron; assault helicopter battalion; two engineer battalions; military police battalion; a detachment from a civil affairs battalion; transportation company; signal battalion; and corps support battalion.

The headquarters itself was far smaller that the 101st's, consisting of only 80 members, all from the I Corps staff or detached from units at Fort Lewis. Whereas MG Petraeus had at his disposal two brigadier generals and numerous colonels, BG Ham only had three colonels: the brigade commander, the TFO chief of staff, and his deputy commander.[21]

Ham and the 3d Brigade Commander, COL Michael Bounds, had to decide where to put their troops after the relief-in-place of the 101st. Since TFO was roughly one-third the size of the 101st, one option would be to replace each 101st brigade with a Stryker battalion of similar type. In the city of Mosul, each sector formerly covered by a 101st battalion would be replaced with a similar TFO Stryker company. Such a deployment had the advantage of providing the same coverage, but at a uniformly reduced level. Disadvantages of such uniformity were, however, that certain places probably required a minimum number of troops that was higher than the reduction would allow. Mosul contained almost two-thirds of the total population of Nineveh Province. A uniform reduction by two-thirds in that city could bring the number of troops there to a dangerously low level. Elsewhere, the command could economize to a level of even greater than two-thirds because the population was less in those areas. Based on this, a second option would be to place roughly the same number of troops in Mosul as the 101st had, and then distribute the remaining forces throughout the country as uniformly as possible. While this option put the troops where most of the people were, it would also leave large parts of northern Iraq with far less coverage than previously.

In deploying the new units, the TFO leadership had to choose between a uniform level for a reduced relief-in-place, or a deployment that weighed certain areas higher than others. Under this option, while the whole TFO deployment was an economy-of-force operation at the theater level, the TFO commander, at his own level, would have to decide whether to have his own economy-of-force within his area of operations.

BG Ham chose the option to weight his forces, with more in Mosul and less in other places. When 3d Brigade elements started arriving in northern Iraq from Samarra in January 2004, four of the TFO's six infantry, cavalry, and field artillery battalions, along with the anti-armor company, were placed in Mosul. The 101st's 2d Brigade had deployed five battalions (four infantry, one field artillery) in Mosul. While the 101st's forces in Mosul represented 26 percent of the division's infantry, cavalry, and field artillery battalions, the TFO commitment to the city represented 66 percent (or two-thirds) of its available battalions of those types. The TFO ratio approximated the size of the Mosul population in comparison to the rest of Nineveh Province.

Elsewhere, TFO/3d Brigade deployed infantry battalions where the 101st previously had brigades. In northwestern Nineveh, centered on Tal Afar, the 101st had deployed a brigade headquarters, three infantry battalions, a field artillery battalion, and an assault helicopter battalion. In its place TFO deployed the 3d Brigade's cavalry squadron. In southern Nineveh, where the 101st used to have a brigade headquarters, two infantry battalions, a cavalry squadron, and a field artillery battalion, TFO deployed a single infantry battalion. In southern Nineveh, the 101st deployed an aviation brigade and two attack and two assault helicopter battalions. TFO replaced this with a single assault helicopter battalion.

Although Ham greatly weighed his deployment to place more troops in Mosul, the TFO forces represented a drastic proportional reduction from those of the 101st, even in Mosul. Across the AO, the American presence was reduced from about 10.41 soldiers per 1,000 inhabitants to a ratio of roughly 4.3 soldiers per 1,000 residents. In Mosul, where the 101st's ratio of combat troops had been the very low 2.4 soldiers per 1,000 city residents, TFO's was 1.8 soldiers per 1,000.[22]

The series of unit relief-in-place actions began in mid-January 2004 and culminated in the handover of the region to Task Force *Olympia* on 5 February 2004. Despite the employment of a lesser amount of troops, things in northern Iraq went smoothly at first. So smoothly that the theater commander, LTG Sanchez, soon began looking to the north for extra troops to use against the Shiite revolt in Najaf. Sanchez was faced with the need for units not only to fight the Shiite revolt, but thereafter as a theater reserve force in case of future crises and to provide theater-wide convoy security. To reshuffle his forces for these missions, Sanchez had several choices concerning TFO.

This included leaving TFO alone and taking the extra forces from other divisions. This choice recognized that TFO was already at a proportionally low strength for its given mission. Taking units away from the north could leave TFO stretched too thin and create places where the insurgents could take advantage of this weakness. On the other hand, however, northern Iraq remained calm, especially compared to places like Fallujah, Najaf, and Baghdad, with radical Sunni and Shiite forces committing themselves to large-scale challenges to Coalition authority.

While reducing TFO ever further was a clear disadvantage, choosing to use TFO units elsewhere for special missions had certain advantages. A Stryker battalion had mobility, firepower, and survivability capabilities that made it a potent unit. The Strykers had already shown their value both in northern Iraq and in Samarra. Additionally, as mentioned above, northern Iraq seemed under control even with the smaller troop levels. A further two ICDC battalions were activated in the spring of 2004, giving the AO a total of six ICDC battalions and another five battalions were in the process of being formed.[23]

In April 2004 when Najaf erupted, Sanchez was ultimately faced with the problem of assembling a suitable reaction force. Northern Iraq was now operating as an economy-of-force AO and Sanchez had to decide whether the use of Strykers elsewhere was worth the risk of reducing TFO even more. Sanchez chose to use the Strykers for other locations in

Iraq. As a result, Task Force *Duke* (TF *Duke*) was created, built around the headquarters of the 3d Brigade, 1st Infantry Division (Mechanized). TF *Duke* consisted of three battalions: a battalion from the 1st Division (2-2d Infantry); a battalion (1st Battalion, 14th Infantry [1-14 IN]) from the 2d Brigade, 25th Infantry Division, which was attached to the 1st Division; and the Stryker-equipped 5-20th Infantry (5-20 IN) from the 3d Brigade, 2d Infantry Division, Task Force *Olympia*. Ironically, the battalion from the 25th Infantry Division, the 1-14 IN, — had just been attached to TFO. This light infantry battalion was sent to Tal Afar to provide extra infantry in that city where the Stryker brigade's cavalry squadron was operating but its 60-day tour there was cut short after only ten days of duty with TFO. Therefore, to the action at Najaf, TFO not only lost one of its three infantry battalions, but also a battalion previously sent to augment its forces.[24]

TF *Duke* assembled in central Iraq, north of Baghdad and then moved to Najaf, south of the Iraqi capital. There, it faced off against the Shiite insurgents for two weeks. The Shiites backed down in order to prevent an expected TF *Duke* assault on the city. The task force was then dissolved and replaced by troops from the nearby 1st Armored Division.[25]

At the time it was dispatched to the south, the 5-20 IN was stationed at Q-West in southern Nineveh Province. The battalion had a company posted farther to the north at Hammam al Alil, one of the few insurgent hotspots in northern Iraq at the time. To replace the battalion, Ham and brigade commander Bounds initially put together an ad hoc battalion-sized force (TF *Sykes*) from various brigade and TFO elements, including the brigade's anti-armor company, a cavalry troop, and an engineer company. When the transfer of the 5-20 IN from Q-West became permanent in June 2004, the TFO command team was forced to decrease the American presence in Mosul to cover the southern outpost. The 1-37th Field Artillery Battalion (1-37 FA) was shifted to Q-West, taking control of the separate anti-armor company, which had been moved to Hammam al Alil under TF Sykes.[26]

TFO's 5-20th IN did not return to its control once the battalion's two-week mission with TF Duke ended. Instead, the Stryker battalion was sent to the 13th Corps Support Command (COSCOM) at the large base near Balad called Logistics Support Area (LSA) Anaconda. From April until June, the battalion performed convoy security operations in central Iraq, where Anti-Iraqi forces (AIF) had been interdicting supply routes. Although the 5-20 IN would return to TFO control in June 2004, its departure in April would mark a permanent reduction in strength of the forces in northern Iraq. For the rest of the Stryker brigade's deployment, one of its battalion-sized units would remain detached to theater control.

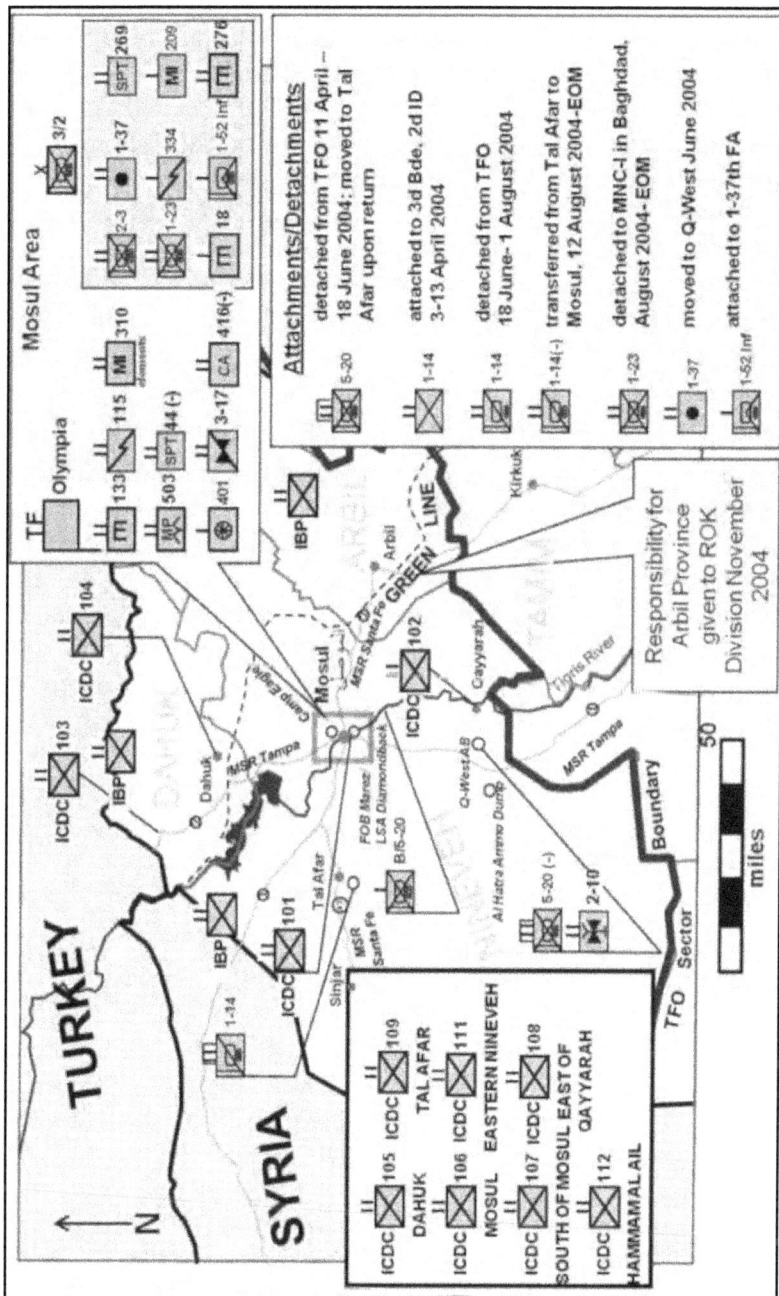

Map 9. Task Force Olympia Deployment in Northern Iraq, 2004

113

The shortage of infantry in Tal Afar was apparent since April 2004 when the 1-14 IN had been briefly assigned there to provide extra foot soldiers. Since its arrival, the TFO unit in the town, the 1st Squadron, 14th Cavalry (1-14 CAV), had swapped its C Troop with 5-20 IN's C Company, to provide infantry for use in the town. An air cavalry troop from TFO's 3-17 CAV was also attached to the 1-14 CAV. In June, the 5-20 IN was relieved from convoy security duties and sent to Tal Afar to provide adequate infantry. However, leaving behind its D Troop attached to the 5-20 IN, the 1-14 CAV was now given that unit's former detached mission. The cavalry squadron remained under 13th COSCOM control until August, when it returned to Tal Afar briefly, before being shifted to Mosul. When the cavalry returned to TFO control, one of the Mosul-based infantry battalions, the 1st Battalion, 23d Infantry (1-23d IN), was detached to serve as the Multi-National Corps Iraq (MNC-I) operational reserve, based in Baghdad, and remained detached for the rest of the Stryker brigade's deployment.[27]

In spite of the optimism displayed by these detachments, the economy-of-force operation in northern Iraq began to face a more volatile situation as the summer of 2004 approached. The most intense fighting in Mosul to date occurred in April. AIF forces concentrated on attacking the local police and the ICDC. The situation had calmed down enough by June when the 1-37 FA was shifted to Q-West but by August the shortage of troops in Mosul began to show. On the 4th, AIF attackers numbering between 30 and 100 insurgents fought Stryker and Iraqi troops with mortars, rocket-propelled grenades (RPGs), small arms, and improvised explosive devices (IEDs) in a series of running battles in which the AIF showed a high degree of coordination. While the ISF bore the brunt, the stakes had been raised in Mosul and Ham and Bounds shifted the cavalry squadron from Tal Afar to the city, where it remained until the brigade rotated home.[28]

Surprising TFO intelligence, the situation in Tal Afar was also deteriorating.[29] Since the arrival of the 5-20 IN to the city in June, US forces had abandoned their outpost, called Rock Base, right in the city. With Iraqi sovereignty restored at that time, local police and security forces were given direct responsibility for Tal Afar. In August TFO conducted its largest operation to date, bringing together parts of all three Stryker infantry battalions, the 5-20th IN, the 1-23 IN (temporarily brought back from MNC-I reserve), and the 2d Battalion, 3d Infantry (2-3 IN), along with three Iraqi National Guard (ING) battalions, the 101st, 102d, and 103d. The ICDC had been redesignated as the Iraqi National Guard in June. These units conducted a large cordon-and-search in Tal Afar and several other towns on successive days. After these operations in early August, the 5-20 IN continued similar activities throughout the month, but the AIF was still potent enough in the city to conduct two large ambushes on 29 August against US forces. The ambushes were foiled, but it was apparent that, in Tal Afar, the insurgency was in control. The local police forces were on the verge of collapse and the Nineveh provincial authorities turned to TFO for help.[30]

Rather than duplicate the previous operation that only targeted specific neighborhoods, BG Ham decided to mount a larger action, Operation BLACK TYPHOON, which would clear the entire city over a period of a week in September. TFO assembled a force of more than 2,000, including the 5-20 IN and 2-3 IN, as well as an ING battalion. With these forces, the city was first completely cordoned off. Prompted by Iraqi authorities, most of the civilian population then evacuated the city. After spending several days bombarding the city with air strikes and artillery, the combined US-Iraqi force next attacked into the center of Tal Afar. Expecting to find and fight a force of roughly 200-300 insurgents, the advance was unopposed. Insurgent resistance had either been destroyed by airstrikes or had escaped the trap. In any event, the city was AIF-free and the civilian population soon returned along with Iraqi government control. However, US forces again withdrew from the city after BLACK TYPHOON. Aside from not wanting to appear as occupiers, Ham stated, "[w]e don't have enough forces to stay in the city."[31]

Despite the raising of two Iraqi divisions in Nineveh, the ING's 2d Division and the Iraqi Army's (IA) 3d Division, the attempt to garrison Nineveh Province with only a single US brigade ended shortly after the 3d Brigade, 2d Infantry Division, redeployed to Fort Lewis in October 2004. The brigade was replaced by another Fort Lewis Stryker unit, the 1st Brigade, 25th Infantry Division. TFO remained in charge until early 2005. Then a staff built around the headquarters of the 11th ACR replaced it, designated Task Force *Freedom*. The TFO area of operations had already been reduced in size in November 2004 when a Republic of Korea (ROK) division took over the Kurdish Arbil Province. Meanwhile, increased AIF activity in Nineveh would result in troop increases there.

During TFO's last few months in Mosul, the city saw its most intense fighting as the AIF attempted to thwart the January 2005 Iraqi constitutional assembly elections. In November 2004, the insurgents mounted a full-scale assault on the ISF. In Sunni western Mosul, the police and some ING units collapsed, forcing the Iraqi government to bring Kurdish ING units into that part of the city for the first time ever. After that, Mosul was reinforced, first with the elite Iraqi 6th Brigade of the Iraqi Intervention Force (IIF), then with several additional US battalions, which remained until after the elections.[32]

Duringthis same period, Tal Afar fared poorly under direct Iraqicontrol. The 200 members of the city police were besieged in the old Ottoman fort in the center of the city that was their headquarters. By April 2005, the city was almost completely under insurgent control once again. The single squadron (4-14 CAV) from the 1st Brigade, 25th Infantry Division, was too small to cope. Accordingly, MNC-I dispatched a brigade-sized unit, the 3d Armored Cavalry Regiment, to Tal Afar.[33]

The 3d ACR was returning for its second tour in Iraq and was originally slated for duty south of Baghdad but the crisis in Tal Afar required its presence there and in April 2005, the regiment deployed to the city. Northern Iraq now had two US brigade-sized forces deployed. By July 2006, the Iraqi 3d Division had taken complete control of operations in northwest Nineveh, including the city of Tal Afar. The 3d ACR conducted a comprehensive, counterinsurgency campaign — Operation RESTORING RIGHTS — that culminated in September 2005 with the ACR and the 3d Iraqi Division clearing the city of insurgents once and for all. When the 3d ACR redeployed in early 2006, northern Iraq became a one-brigade AO once again.[34]

However, at this point, things had changed throughout Nineveh Province. In the eastern part of the province, the 1st Brigade, 25th Infantry Division, followed by the 172d Infantry Brigade (another Stryker unit), obtained similar, if less dramatic, results to those of the 3d ACR in Tal Afar. By mid-2006, the Iraqi 2d Division had taken the lead in Mosul, Q-West, and eastern Nineveh. With the Iraqis in charge, when the 172d Brigade was relieved by the 3d Brigade, 2d Infantry Division, on its second tour in Mosul, the returning brigade dispatched one-third of its combat power (1-14 Cav and 1-23 IN) to Baghdad to reinforce US units there.[35]

The replacement of a division by a brigade in northern Iraq in 2004 was a deliberate economy-of-force measure. An observer from the 101st lamented that the smaller deployments after his division left Iraq did not allow the follow-on troops the ability to network on a daily basis with Iraqi officials and the public.[36] However, given the timing and overall situation, there were simply few other options available to US deployment planners and decision makers. Immediately after OIF I, there were too few available units to replace the 101st with another division. And northern Iraq was the only relatively calm section of Iraq where US troops deployed. After doing more with less for most of 2004, reinforcements were ultimately dispatched to Nineveh Province. The success in the province in 2005 resulted in the ability to withdraw troops from the province in 2006, placing US forces below a brigade in size.

Notes

1. BG Carter F. Ham, 2006, interview by Peter Connors, 28 June 2006, Fort Leavenworth; "101st Airborne Division Transfers Authority to Task Force Olympia," United States Central Command Press Release Number 04-02-08, 5 February 2004, online at http://www.globalsecurity.org/military/ library/news/2004/02/mil-040205-centcom01.htm, accessed on 21 September 2006.

2. Only Nineveh Province was originally included in the 101st's area of responsibility, with Arbil and Dahuk falling under the supervision of Army Special Forces. See Kirsten Lundberg, "The Accidental Statesman: GEN Petraeus and the City of Mosul, Iraq," Kennedy School of Government Case Program C15-06-1834.0, John F. Kennedy School of Government, Harvard University, Cambridge, MA, 2006, 3.

3. "Iraq: Administrative Divisions (Population and Area)," *World Gazetteer*, online at http://world-gazetteer.com/r/r_iq.htm; Internet, accessed on 2 October 2006.

4. Lundberg; COL Joseph Anderson, 2005, interview by Catherine Small, 4 November 2006, Fort Leavenworth.

5. The troop density per 1,000, based on historical experience, is 13.26. See John J. McGrath, *Boots on the Ground: Troop Density in Contingency Operations* (Fort Leavenworth: US Army Combat Studies Institute, 2006), 109.

6. The 3d Battalion, 327th Infantry, usually assigned to the 1st Brigade, was attached to the 2d Brigade and operated in Mosul.

7. COL Gregory Gass and MAJ John White, 2005, interview by Catherine Small, 31 October 2005, Fort Leavenworth.

8. "101st Division Artillery," *Field Artillery Journal* (November-December 2004): 39; LTC Henry A. Arnold, 2005, interview by the Operational Leadership Experiences Project Team with the Combat Studies Institute, 21 October 2005, Fort Leavenworth, 12, 14; Robert Woodward, "101st, 3rd ACR Root Out Terrorists, Insurgents," *Iraqi Destiny* 1 (11 December 2003): 5,10. In addition to the battalions from the 3d Brigade watching the border with Syria, Company F, 51st Infantry, a long- range surveillance unit attached to the 101st's 311th Military Intelligence Battalion was also conducting security operations along the border with Iran and Turkey. See Joshua Hutcheson, "First Iran Border Control Point Opened," *Iraqi Destiny* 1 (31 October 2003): 4; Lundberg, 54.

9. "101st Corps Support Group Reopens Tall Kayf Girls Secondary School," *Iraqi Destiny* 1 (31 October 2003): 7; Anderson interview; Thomas Day, "Nebraska Principal, Guardsman Works to Improve Iraqi School System," *Iraqi Destiny* 1 (31 October 2003): 6; Lundberg, 27, 54, 57; COL David C. Martino,2005, interview by Lynne Chandler Garcia, 18 December 2005, Fort Leavenworth. On page 57 of Lundberg may be found the original list of the function responsibilities parceled out within the 101st.

10. LTC Michael Shenk, 2005, interview by the Operational Leadership Experiences Project Team with the Combat Studies Institute, 15 February 2005, Fort Leavenworth.

11. Donald C. Fryc, "Iraqi Security Company Formation," *Iraqi Destiny* 1 (17 July 2003): 2; "Mosul Camp Integrates Security Forces," *Iraqi Destiny* 1 (17 July 2003): 11; Joshua Hutcheson, "101st Helps Celebrate Iraqi Army Birthday," *Iraqi Destiny* 1 (15 January 2004): 2; Arnold interview, 12.

12. Bill Putnam, "Keane Announces Unit Rotation Schedule," *Iraqi Destiny* 1 (24 July 2003): 3; "Gen. Keane Press Briefing on Plan to Rotate Forces in Iraq," 23 January 2003, online at http://www.globalsecurityorg/military/library/news/2003/07/mil-030723-dod03, accessed on 21 September 2006.

13. Jim Garamore, "Planning for Replacing Troops in Iraq," *American Forces Press Service*, 16 October 2003, online at http://www.defenselink.mil/ news/Oct2003/n10162003_200310168.html; Internet; accessed on 21 September 2006; Richard L. Armitage, 2006, interview by Pete Connors, 29 June 2006, Fort Leavenworth.

14. Using US Marine forces was out of the question. Marine forces were fully committed to supporting the deployment to Anbar Province and the shorter Marine rotation terms (7 months versus the Army's 12 months), would have made such a transition difficult at best..

15. The division headquarters that recently redeployed or were about to do so were the 1st Armored, 3d, 4th, 10th Mountain, 29th (ARNG), 82d Airborne, and, of course, the 101st Airborne. The division headquarters deployed, or about to be deployed, were the 1st, 1st Cavalry, and the 25th. The ARNG division head- quarters not mobilized yet were the 28th, 34th, 35th, 36th (which was just forming), 38th, 40th, and 42d.

16. The brigades that recently redeployed or were about to do so were the three brigades of the 1st Armored Division, 3d Infantry Division, 4th Infantry Division, and 101st Airborne Division, respectively, as well as a brigade from the 10th Mountain Division; two brigades from the 82d Airborne Division; the 173d Airborne Brigade; the ARNG's 53d, 76th Infantry Brigades and the 66th Brigade, 35th Infantry Division; the 2d Light Cavalry Regiment; and the 3d and 278th (ARNG) ACRs. The ARNG brigades not mobilized yet were two brigades of the 28th and 38th Infantry Divisions respectively; three brigades each of the 29th, 36th 40th, and 42d Infantry Divisions; one brigade from each of the 34th and 35th Infantry Divisions; the 27th, 29th, 32d, 41st, 48th, 76th, 92d, 218th, and 256th Infantry Brigades; the 115th Armored Brigade, and the 116th Cavalry Brigade. The brigades in training, which were preparing for a scheduled deployment, were the 2d Brigade, 10th Mountain Division; the 1st Brigade, 25th Infantry Division; 2d Brigade, 34th Infantry Division; the 37th Brigade, 38th Infantry Division; and the 172d Infantry Brigade. The brigades deployed or about to be deployed were the three brigades of the 1st Infantry Division; the three brigades of the 1st Cavalry Division; two brigades of the 25th Infantry

Division; one brigade of the 82d Airborne Division; the 56th Brigade, 28th Infantry Division; the 3d Brigade, 2d Infantry Division, and the 30th, 39th, 45th, and 81st Infantry Brigades. A brigade from the 2d Infantry Division in Korea and the headquarters of the 11th ACR were eventually sent to Iraq for OIF-III.

17. Garamore.

18. Dan Murphy, "US to begin drawdown in Iraq: In coming weeks, 18,000 troops in northern Iraq will be replaced with a force half that size." Christian Science Monitor, 4 January 2004, online at http://www.csmonitor.com/2004/0115/p01s04-woiq.html, accessed on 22 September 2006.

19. Ham interview, 4; "101st Airborne Division Transfers Authority to Task Force Olympia," United States Central Command Press Release Number 04-02-08, 5 February 2004, online at http://www.globalsecurity.org/military/library/news/2004/02/mil-040205-centcom01.htm, accessed on 21 September 2006. The ICDC battalions were the 101st, 102d, 103d, and 104th battalions. The 101st and 102d were Sunni units raised in Mosul and Qayyarah, respectively. The 103d and 104th were Kurdish units in Dahuk province. The designations of the three IBP battalions is unknown, but there were one each in Nineveh, Dahuk, and Arbil provinces by early 2004; Murphy.

20. Ham interview, 2-3; "Operational Update from the Multinational Brigade Commander," 9 March 2004, online at http://www.defenselink.mil/tran- scripts/2004/tr20040309-0522.html, accessed on 8 October 2006.

21. Ham interview, 3, 5.

22. The historical base for troop density is 13.26 per 1,000 of population. See McGrath, *Boots on the Ground*. The figures used to develop these ratios were as follows: 101st strength, 25,000; TFO strength, 10,000; 101st strength in Mosul: 4,000 (5 battalions x 800 personnel); TFO strength in Mosul: 3,200 (4 battalions x 800 personnel); Nineveh Province population: 2.4 million; Mosul population: 1.7 million.

23. Doug Sample, "Task Force Commander Says Insurgents 'Desperate, Isolated,'" *American Forces Information Service*, online at http://www.defenselink. mil/news/Mar2004/n03092004_200403095.html, accessed on 8 October 2006.

24. William Cole, "Hawaii Troops Shifted to Volatile Mosul Area," *Honolulu Advertiser*, 7 April 2004, online at http://the.honoluluadvertiser.com/dispatch-es/ stories/040704, accessed 20 September 2006; William Cole, "Golden Dragons Display Quick-Strike Capabilities," *Honolulu Advertiser*, 13 April 2004 online at http://the.honoluluadvertiser.com/dispatches/stories/041304, accessed on 7 October 2006.

25. Kimberly Snow, "V Corps Brigade Moves to Help Keep Peace in An Najaf," online at http://www.vcorps.army.mil/news/2004/may10_najaf.htm, accessed on 6 October 2006.

26. Steven Silwa, "Maneuver and the Other Missions in OIF: 1-37 FA 3/2 SBCT," *Field Artillery* (March-April 2005): 10-14. The 1-37 left a battery behind in Mosul to guard the division headquarters.

27. Kevin G. Hosier, "1-14th Cavalry Squadron 'Warhorse,'" *The Arrowhead:* [3d Brigade, 2d Infantry Division] *Family Readiness Group Newsletter* 5 (22 January 2004): 7-8; Buddy Carman, "1st Squadron, 14th US Cavalry WAR-HORSE! Operation Iraqi Freedom Operations Summary & Update," online at http://www.14cav.org/114update.html, accessed on 6 October 2006. The 1-23 IN included a troop from the 1-14 CAV. The battalion was briefly returned to northern Iraq in September 2004 to participate in Operation BLACK TYPHOON, the clearing of Tal Afar. MNC-I was one of two new commands, the other being the Multinational Forces-Iraq (MNF-I), which replaced CJTF-7 in mid-2004.

28. Ham interview, 6; "Coordinated Attacks in Mosul Leave 14 Civilians Dead," Task Force Olympia Press Release, 4 August 2004, online at http://www.strykernews.com/archives/2004/08/04/coordinated_attacks_in_mosul_leave_14_civilians_dead.html, accessed on 8 October 2006; Michael Gilbert, "Stryker Brigade Slammed by Insurgents," *The* [Tacoma, WA] *News Tribune*, 10 August 2004, online at http://www.strykernews.com/archives/2004/08/10/ stryker_brigade_slammed_by_insurgents.html#more, accessed on 8 October 2006.

29. Steve Fainaru, "After Recapturing N. Iraqi City, Rebuilding Starts from Scratch," *Washington Post*, 19 September 2004: p. A32, online at http://www.washingtonpost.com/ac2/wp-dyn/A31377-2004Sep18?language=printer, accessed on 20 September 2006.

30. Michael Gilbert, "Stryker Unit Notes Successes, Readies to Head Home, *"The* [Tacoma, WA] *News Tribune*, 16 August 2004, online at http://www. strykernews.com/archives/2004/09/16/stryker_unit_notes_successes_readies_ to_head_home.html#more, accessed on 8 October 2006; Fred Minnick, "Three Operations in Three Days," 19 August 2004, article archived on *Stryker Brigade News*, online at http://www.strykernews.com/archives/2004/08/19/ three_operations_in_three_days.html#more, accessed on 8 October 2006; "Anti-Iraqi Forces Attack Two MNF Convoys Injuring 34 Civilians," Task Force Olympia Press Release, 29 August 2004, online at http://www.strykernews.com/ archives/2004/08/29/antiiraqi_forces_attack_two_mnf_convoys_injuring_34_ ci- vilians.html#more, accessed on 8 October 2006.

31. Rick Jervis, "US Military Encounters New N. Front in Tal Afar," *Chicago Tribune*, 14 September 2004, online at available at http://www.strykernews. com/archives/2004/09/14/us_military_encounters_new_n_front_in_tal_afar. html#more, accessed on 8 October 2006; Gilbert, "Stryker Unit Notes Successes, Readies to Head Home;" Steve Fainaru, "US-Led Forces Retake Northern Iraqi City," *Washington Post*, 13 September 2004: p. A17, online at http://www. washingtonpost.com/wp-dyn/articles/A16793-2004Sep12.html, accessed on 8 October 2006; Fainaru, "After Recapturing N. Iraqi City, Rebuilding Starts From Scratch."

32. The IIF remained until May 2005, when it was replaced by the now trained 2d Iraqi Division. In January 2005, the ING, IIF, and Iraqi Army were merged into a force called the Iraqi Army. The main difference between former ING units and the IIF and old Iraqi Army were that ING units were recruited locally, while IA/IIF units were recruited nationally. Therefore the 2d Division, formerly ING, which ultimately ended up as the Iraqi garrison in Mosul, was composed of local Sunni and Kurdish units. On the other hand, the 3d Division, an IA unit, which later garrisoned the Tal Afar area, was composed of an ethnic mix of the overall population. Among the US reinforcements in Mosul in early 2005 was the 1-14 IN, which had previously served briefly in Tal Afar.

33. "Tall 'Afar," *GlobalSecurity.org*, online at http://www.globalsecurity. org/ military/world/iraq/tall-afar.htm, accessed on 9 October 2006.

34. Christopher Hickey, "Letter to Squadron Families," 4 May 2005; Thomas E. Ricks, "The Lessons of Counterinsurgency: US Unit Praised for Tactics Against Iraqi Fighters, Treatment of Detainees," *Washington Post*, 16 February 2006, p. A14, online at http://www.washingtonpost.com/wp-dyn/content/arti-cle/2006/02/15/AR2006021502586_pf.htm, accessed on 8 October 2006; COL Michael Shields, Pentagon Press Briefing, 21 July 2006, online at http://www. mnf-iraq.com/index.php?option=com_content&task= view&id=1121&Itemid=3 1&lang=arabic, Internet; accessed on 27 September 2006.

35. Shields interview; Sean Cockerham, "Same War, Different Duty, *The* [Tacoma, WA] *News Tribune*, 8 October 2006, online at http://www.thenewstri-bune.com/news/military/stryker/story/6149856p-5382489c.html, accessed on 9 October 2006. The tour of the 172d Brigade was extended and the brigade was also sent to Baghdad in the summer of 2006.

36. Anderson interview.

Glossary

1LT	first lieutenant
1SG	first sergeant
2LT	second lieutenant
ACR	Armored Cavalry Regiment
ADA	Air Defense Artillery
AIF	Anti-Iraqi Forces
AO	area of operations
AOR	area of responsibility
ARNG	Army National Guard
BCT	Brigade Combat Team
BDE	brigade
BG	brigadier general
Bn	battalion
CA	Civil Affairs
CPT	captain
CAV	Cavalry
CJTF-7	Combined Joint Task Force-7
COL	colonel
CONOP	Contingency Operation
COP	combat outpost
COSCOM	Corps Support Command
CP	command post
CPL	corporal
CSM	command sergeant major
DOD	Department of Defense
FA	Field Artillery
FIST	Fire Support Team
FLA	front line ambulance
FOB	Forward Operating Base
FRE	Former Regime Element
GEN	general
HEAT	high explosive antitank (round)
HHC	Headquarters and Headquarters Company

HMMWV	high mobility multi-purpose wheeled vehicle
HVT	high-value target
IA	Iraqi Army
IBP	Iraqi Border Police
ICDC	Iraqi Civil Defense Corps
ID	Infantry Division
IED	improvised explosive device
IIF	Iraqi Intervention Force
IN	Infantry
ING	Iraqi National Guard
INP	Iraqi National Police
IO	Information Operations
ISF	Iraqi Security Forces
ISU	integrated sight unit
JISC	Joint Iraqi Security Company
JRTC	Joint Readiness Training Center
KIA	killed in action
LSA	logistics support area
LTC	lieutenant colonel
LTG	lieutenant general
MAJ	major
MiTT	Military Transition Team
MG	major general
MGS	Mobile Gun System
MNC-I	Multinational Corps-Iraq
MND-W	Multinational Division-West
MNF-N	Multinational Force-North
MSG	master sergeant
MSR	main supply route
NTC	National Training Center
ODA	Operational Detachment Alpha
OIF	Operation IRAQI FREEDOM

OIF I	First Rotation, Operation IRAQI FREEDOM, 2003-2004
OIF II	Second Rotation, Operation IRAQI FREEDOM, 2004-2005
OIF III	Third Rotation, Operation IRAQI FREEDOM, 2005-2006
OPFOR	opposing forces
PFC	private first class
QRF	Quick Reaction Force
Q-West	Qayyarah West Airfield
ROK	Republic of Korea
RPG	rocket propelled grenade
RTO	Radio-Telephone Operator
S-1	personnel officer
S-2	intelligence officer
S-3	operations officer
SAW	squad automatic weapon
SECDEF	Secretary of Defense
SFC	sergeant first class
SGM	sergeant major
SGT	sergeant
SOF	Special Operations Forces
SPC	specialist
SSG	staff sergeant
TAA	tactical assembly area
TAC	Tactical Command Post
TCP	traffic control point
TF	Task Force
TFO	Task Force Olympia
TOC	Tactical Operations Center
TOW	tube-launched optically-tracked wire-guided missile
UAV	unmanned aerial vehicle
US	United States
VBIED	vehicle-borne improvised explosive device
WIA	wounded in action
XO	executive officer

About the Contributors

Thomas A. Bruscino, Jr., worked at the US Army Center of Military History in Washington, DC, before joining the Combat Studies Institute in 2005. He is an assistant professor in the US Army's School of Advanced Military Studies, Command and General Staff College, Fort Leavenworth. Dr. Bruscino earned his BA in history from Adams State College in Alamosa, Colorado, in 1999, his MA in American history from Ohio University in 2002, and his Ph.D. in American military history in 2005. He is the author of several CSI works and his articles and review essays have appeared in the *Claremont Review of Books*, *Journal of America's Past*, *San Luis Valley Historian*, and *Reviews in American History*. His book, *A Nation Forged in War: How World War II Taught Americans to Get Along*, was published in 2010 by the University of Tennessee Press. He was also co-general editor of *Population-Centric Counterinsurgency: A False Idol? Three Monographs from the School of Advanced Military Studies*, published by CSI Press in 2011.

Matt M. Matthews joined the US Army Combat Studies Institute in July 2005 after working for 16 years as a member of the Battle Command Training Program at Fort Leavenworth. Mr. Matthews graduated from Kansas State University in 1986 with a BS in History. After serving on active duty in the Army as an enlisted man from 1977 to 1981, he served as an officer in the Army Reserve and Kansas Army National Guard from 1983 to 1991. Mr. Matthews has co-authored numerous scholarly articles on the Civil War in the Trans-Mississippi and has written several CSI publications, including *The Posse Comitatus Act and the United States Army: A Historical Perspective; Operation AL FAJR: A Study in Army and Marine Joint Operations; The US Army on the Mexican Border: A Historical Perspective; We Were Caught Unprepared: The 2006 Hezbollah War;* and *An Ever Present Danger: A Concise History of British Military Operations on the North-West Frontier, 1849-1947.* His has also contributed studies for *Vanguard of Valor: Small Unit Actions in Afghanistan,* Volumes I and II.

John J. McGrath has worked for the US Army Combat Studies Institute (CSI) as an Army historian since December 2002. He also served as an Army historian for more than four years at the US Army Center of Military History from 1998 to 2002. He has worked for or served in the United States Army since 1978. Mr. McGrath worked full-time for the Army Reserve in Massachusetts for 15 years, both as an active duty reservist and as a civilian military technician. In the former capacity in 1991 he served in Saudi Arabia with the 22d Support Command during Operation DESERTSTORM as the command historian. He has a BA from Boston College, an MA from the University of Massachusetts at Boston, and is a Ph.D. history candidate at Kansas State University. Mr. McGrath is the author of numerous articles and military history publications, including *Theater Logistics in the Gulf War*, published by the Army Materiel Command in 1994, and seven books published by the CSI Press, the most recent being 2010's *Wanat: Combat Action in Afghanistan, 2008*. He also has contributed to several anthologies produced and published by CSI and has been the general editor of two collected works.

www.ingramcontent.com/pod-product-compliance
Lightning Source LLC
Chambersburg PA
CBHW050353100426

42739CB00015BB/3388